THE
TOP 100
FINGER FOODS
FOR BABIES & TODDLERS

THE

TOP 100
FINGER FOODS
FOR BABIES & TODDLERS

Christine Bailey

DELICIOUS, HEALTHY MEALS FOR YOUR CHILD TO ENJOY

DUNCAN BAIRD PUBLISHERS

LONDON

The Top 100 Finger Foods For Babies & Toddlers
Christine Bailey

First published in the United Kingdom and Ireland in 2012 by
Duncan Baird Publishers Ltd
Sixth Floor, Castle House
75–76 Wells Street, London W1T 3QH

Conceived, created and designed by Duncan Baird Publishers

Managing Editor: Grace Cheetham
Editor: Alison Bolus
Managing Designer: Manisha Patel
Designer: Luana Gobbo
Commissioned Photography: Simon Smith
Food Stylist: Mari Williams
Prop Stylist: Lucy Harvey

British Library Cataloguing-in-Publication Data:
A CIP record for this book is available from the British Library

ISBN: 978-1-84899-011-1

10 9 8 7 6 5 4 3 2 1

Typeset in Helvetica
Colour reproduction by Brightarts
Printed in China by Imago

My sincere thanks go to Grace Cheetham for
commissioning me to write this great book.
Thank you also to my amazing editor, Alison
Bolus, for all her tireless patience, support and
feedback. I would also like to thank my wonderful
husband, Chris, and my three fantastic children,
Nathan, Isaac and Simeon, for tasting every
recipe numerous times and providing me with
plenty of inspiration, love and support.

Publisher's Note
The information in this book is not intended as a substitute for
professional medical advice and treatment. If you are pregnant
or breastfeeding, or have any special dietary requirements or
medical conditions, it is recommended that you consult a
medical professional before following any of the information
or recipes contained in this book. Duncan Baird Publishers,
or any other persons who have been involved in working on
this publication, cannot accept responsibility for any errors
or omissions, inadvertent or not, that may be found in the
recipes or text, or for any problems that may arise as a result
of preparing one of these recipes or following the advice
contained in this work.

Notes on the Recipes
Unless otherwise stated:
Use medium eggs, fruit and vegetables
Use fresh ingredients, including herbs and chillies
Do not mix metric and imperial measurements
1 tsp = 5ml   1 tbsp = 15ml   1 cup = 250ml

Symbols are used to identify even small amounts of an
ingredient. Where optional ingredients are listed, the symbols
reflect both ingredients, so a recipe using olive oil, with
coconut oil as an alternative, will not show the "nut-free"
symbol, in case the reader chooses the alternative. Dairy
foods may include cow's, goat's or sheep's milk. Check the
manufacturer's labelling to ensure cheeses are vegetarian.
Give only the relevantly identified foods to those children with
a food allergy or intolerance.

contents

KEY TO SYMBOLS

Suitable for Vegetarians These recipes contain no meat, poultry, fish, seafood or animal byproducts, like gelatine.

Suitable for Vegans These recipes do not contain any meat, poultry, fish, seafood or other animal-derived ingredients, such as animal fats and gelatine. They also contain no eggs, dairy products or honey.

Gluten-free These recipes contain no gluten – a protein found in wheat, rye and barley as well as products containing these grains.

Wheat-free These recipes avoid any wheat grain or wheat-derived products – a common allergen.

Egg-free These recipes do not contain any egg or egg-based products.

Dairy-free These recipes do not include any dairy products, including cow's milk, sheep's milk and goat's milk, and products derived from them.

Nut-free These recipes do not contain any nuts or nut-derived products. You may be able to substitute nuts with seeds.

Seed-free These recipes do not contain any seeds, or their oils.

Soya-free These recipes do not contain soya or soya-based products, such as tofu, soy sauce, miso or soya milk.

Sugar-free In this book, the label "sugar-free" refers to food that is naturally sweetened with fruit only. I use xylitol as a sweetener in many recipes, but have classified it as a sugar.

INTRODUCTION

Every parent instinctively wants the best for their child. We want to help them grow up to be intelligent, happy and healthy, fully equipped to live their lives to the full. It is during childhood that they experience the most rapid growth and development, physically, mentally and emotionally. So if we're looking to maximize their potential, it is essential that we ensure that they are optimally nourished. The period between birth and 5 years is one of rapid growth and development, when children's energy demands soar as they become more independent. To fuel all of this activity, they need nutrient-dense foods in a form that will appeal to their little mouths and hands. This is where finger foods can be so important. By providing children with a wide range of nutrient-dense bite-sized foods, you can introduce them to new tastes and textures, encourage independent eating and nourish their active bodies.

ABOUT THIS BOOK

This book provides you with nutritional information on which foods to include in your child's diet, as well as featuring 100 delicious finger food recipes. The recipes are designed with pre-school children in mind, including many to tempt your little baby to start eating finger foods, but are equally suitable for older children and adults. Each recipe is packed with nutrients to optimize your child's growth and development, support immune health and provide essential nutrients for brain function. All the recipes are designed with our busy lifestyles in mind: most are quick and easy to prepare, with many suitable for freezing. There are also recipes that are free from a variety of common allergens, and plenty of vegetarian and vegan options.

NUTRITIONAL NEEDS OF TODDLERS

Depending on their age, size and activity level, toddlers and pre-school children need around 1000–1500 calories a day. In addition to meeting their energy requirements, nutrient needs are particularly high as they reach various developmental milestones. Growth is an important physiological process during this age range, but, in addition, children's bodies are undergoing a number of changes internally. Their immune system is still relatively immature, and organs such as lungs and the digestive system are still developing. The brain is growing at a rapid rate. In fact, the brain increases in size by around 50% between the ages of one and five years. In addition, however, toddlers have made the transition from being fed to feeding themselves. This is a crucial time when they start to develop preferences and attitudes about food that can greatly influence the quality of the food they eat and the nutrients they receive.

In view of their small size, pre-school children can find it difficult to eat sufficient amounts of food at any one time to fulfil their high nutritional needs, so all meals and snacks should be nutrient dense.

THE ESSENTIAL BUILDING BLOCKS

During children's early years and beyond, it is important to ensure their diet is varied and contains all the key elements for growth and development. These macronutrients – protein, carbohydrates and healthy fats – are the essential building blocks for a healthy diet.

Protein

Protein provides amino acids, the building blocks of the body. These are vital for the development of the skeletal structure, including bones, cartilage, ligaments, teeth and nails, as well as the body's hormonal system, development of new muscle, organ tissue and neurotransmitters – the chemical messengers of the brain. Deficiency in amino acids can influence growth and development as well as affect behaviour, memory and concentration.

The quality of a protein is determined by its balance of amino acids. Though there are 23 amino acids from which the body can build everything, only eight are considered essential because these can come only through the diet, whilst the others can be made by the body. All animal products (meat, dairy, eggs, fish, seafood) provide these eight amino acids, whereas vegetables sources (with the exception of foods such as soya, quinoa and green superfoods, for example chlorella and spirulina) are incomplete. Therefore, with a vegetarian diet it is necessary to include a wide range of different vegetable sources in the daily diet.

Protein requirements are calculated as the amount in grams per kilograms of body weight. For a one to three year old this is around 0.94g/kg per day. For a three year old this would be around 13g. For older children (four to eight years) it would rise to around 19g. To ensure sufficient protein, your child needs to eat two to three servings of protein a day. As a general guide, 30g meat or fish provides around 7g protein. A serving size looks like 2–4 tablespoons of grated cheese, 1 egg, 2 tablespoons of fish or meat or 2–5 tablespoons of beans.

Carbohydrates

To fuel their rapid growth and development, children need adequate amounts of carbohydrate. Carbohydrate-rich foods, such as fruits, vegetables, bread, pasta, rice and potatoes, are broken down into glucose during digestion. The glucose is then absorbed into the bloodstream. For sustained energy, it is vital that the supply of glucose remains even throughout the day. Refined carbohydrates and sugary foods, such as white bread, rice, biscuits, cakes and sugary drinks, are broken down quickly by the body, causing a rapid rise in blood sugar levels. This results in insulin being released, and the resulting dip in blood sugar will cause your child to feel irritable and moody, to lack concentration and crave more sugar. The result is see-sawing blood sugar levels.

To ensure more balanced blood sugar levels, choose carbohydrates that release glucose slowly into the bloodstream, such as vegetables, beans and pulses, fresh fruit and whole grains. You can also use something called the Glycemic Load (GL). This measures the effect of a food on blood glucose levels. Foods with a low score (below 10) should form the main carbohydrates in your child's diet, and foods with scores of 11–14 eaten in moderation. Examples of moderate and low GL foods include whole grains, oats, vegetables, beans or lentils and fruits such as berries, plums, pears, apples and citrus fruits. One way to keep a meal balanced is to include some protein or healthy fat with a carbohydrate food, as this can slow down how quickly glucose is released. For example, a slice of wholegrain toast with nut butter is a better option than a slice of wholegrain toast with honey. Although whole grains are nutritious, too many can fill children up too quickly without providing sufficient calories or nutrients for their needs. As their digestive systems are still immature, too many grains can cause digestive upsets as well as being potential allergens. It is healthier to focus more on vegetables, which are gentler on the digestive system and nutrient rich. Whilst some fruits are faster releasing than others, eating whole fresh fruit is better than drinking fruit juice. Whole fruits provide soluble fibre, which slows down the release of sugars found in the fruit. Fruits are also rich in vitamins, minerals and antioxidants, which are important for your child's health. Dried fruit (a concentrated source of sugar) should be eaten only in small quantities.

Portion size ranges

Toddler appetites vary from meal to meal and day to day, so a portion size range is generally recommended. Sometimes children eat very small portions of food, especially if they are tired or unwell. At other times they may eat larger portions, for example after a lot of active play. Offering a nutrient-rich diet and allowing children to eat to their appetite is the best strategy. Each day aim for your toddler to be eating at least two pieces of fruit plus four servings of vegetables. As a simple guide, a serving is ½–1 piece of fruit, such as an apple or clementine, ½–1 tablespoon vegetables or around four florets (e.g. broccoli). For grains, a serving is around 2–5 tablespoons cooked pasta or rice, ½–1 slice of bread, or 1–3 tablespoons mashed potato, with around half of this being whole grains. When planning a meal, aim for half their plate to be full of vegetables, a quarter protein-rich foods and the remaining quarter starchy carbohydrates, such as potatoes or grains.

Essential Fats

Fat gets a lot of bad press, but the truth is that the right types of fats are essential for your child's health. Fat plays an important role in the provision of energy as well as being crucial for the maturation of organs, immune function and building a healthy brain. But your child needs the right kind of fat in the right quantities.

Essential fats – the omega-3 and omega-6 fatty acids (polyunsaturated fats) – are particularly important for the development of the brain and body systems, including the nervous system, hormonal system and digestive tract. Insufficiency in these fats can lead to dry, flaky skin, dry hair and dandruff and itchy eyes as well as poor memory, short attention span, mood swings and concentration problems. The other types of fats include saturated fats, monounsaturated fats and cholesterol. These fats can be made by the body, unlike the essential omega fats, which have to be supplied through the diet. Therefore focus on providing sufficient omega fats in your child's diet and in particular omega-3 fats, which are often deficient in children's diets.

The omega-3 parent fatty acid is known as alpha-linolenic acid (ALA) and is converted by the body into the metabolically active EPA (eicosapentaenoic acid) and DHA (docosahexaenoic acid). However, this conversion is inefficient, so it is important to include foods that provide a direct source of EPA and DHA, such as oily fish (for example salmon, sardines, mackerel, herring, trout, halibut, anchovies). One caution however: larger oily fish, such as tuna, shark and marlin, tend to be higher in heavy metals and pesticides than small oily fish, and so are best avoided. Tinned tuna is also not a good source of omega-3 fats, as the canning process removes most of them. The omega-3 content of farmed fish depends on the quality of their diet, so, where possible, opt for wild, sustainably caught oily fish, such as Alaskan salmon, or organic farmed fish. Another souce of omega-3 fats is seeds such as linseed, hemp or pumpkin seeds. But since the conversion process of ALA to EPA and DHA from seeds is inefficient, a supplement may be appropriate for vegetarians (see p.18).

Fat provides a useful source of energy in a child's diet, so it is recommended that around 30% of their total calorie intake should be fat, with no more than one-third saturated fat and at least one-third essential fats. Damaged or hydrogenated fats found in processed or fried foods and some margarines are harmful for health and should not figure in your child's diet. A low-fat diet is also not recommended for young children, as it will not provide sufficient calories and can be lower in valuable fat-soluble vitamins, such as vitamin D. It is recommended that children under one year should drink breast or formula milk, with organic whole cow's milk or alternatives for recipes, and children under two should have whole milk. Semi-skimmed milk or milk alternatives are recommended for children from two.

To ensure the presence of sufficient omega fats, aim for your child to eat fish three times a week, focusing on oily fish, and include seeds or seed oils daily. Seed oils such as flaxseed and hemp seed are readily available and can be useful for adding to dressings, dips and spreads or poured over warm foods, but must not be heated. Other good sources include walnuts, chia seeds, pumpkin seeds, tofu, leafy green vegetables, such as broccoli and kale, and organic or omega-3-rich eggs.

Careful choices need to be made when cooking with oils. Whilst omega-3 and 6 fats are essential for your child's health, they are also prone to damage by cooking, heating and food processing and so not suitable as a cooking oil. The best oils to use when cooking are organic coconut oil, which is less prone to damage on heating, or olive oil.

Polyunsaturated oils (for example vegetable oils such as corn, soya and sunflower) are not recommended for use because they will rapidly form trans-fats when heated.

Vitamins and Minerals

The entire range of vitamins and minerals is essential for the growth and health of your child, because children have high nutrient demands and generally low stores of these micronutrients.

However, national dietary surveys highlight the often limited range of foods eaten by toddlers, making them vulnerable to vitamin and mineral deficiencies. A range of vitamins and minerals, for example, are required for brain function, including B vitamins, folic acid, vitamin C, magnesium, manganese and zinc. The B vitamins are particularly important because the brain uses vast amounts of them. Good sources include whole grains, leafy green vegetables, lean meat, fish and eggs.

Antioxidants are important to help protect your child's brain and body from harmful oxidants known as free radicals. These can damage your child's cells and tissues, affecting the function and health of body systems and impairing immune function. Constant exposure to free radicals in our environment, fried and processed foods and additives means that your child's requirements for antioxidants on a daily basis are high. Key antioxidants include beta-carotene, vitamin C, vitamin E, selenium, glutathione, coenzyme Q10 and phytonutrients – plant compounds present in fresh fruits and vegetables. One of the best ways to ensure a good daily intake is to include a colourful selection of fruits and vegetables.

Vitamin D plays an important role in many body systems, including bone health and immune function. However, Vitamin D deficiency is increasingly common in children. The main source of vitamin D is sunlight. Food sources are limited and include fortified foods, eggs and oily fish. A vitamin D supplement of 400ius daily, available as drops, sprays and tablets, is recommended for children under five.

Calcium and magnesium are also essential for bone health, and toddlers should ingest around 450mg calcium and 120mg magnesium daily. A 150g/5oz carton of natural yogurt contains around 200–250mg calcium, and 250ml/9fl oz calcium-fortified alternative milk or semi-skimmed milk contains about 300mg. So 2–3 servings a day are sufficient to meet requirements. Other useful sources of calcium include canned fish, tofu, almonds, tahini and leafy vegetables.

Iron deficiency can be a common problem in young children. Too little iron can slow the growth of children, lead to low energy levels and increase susceptibility to infection. It is also vital for the developing brain and cognitive function. Good iron-rich foods include leafy green vegetables, lean meats, eggs, beans and pulses, dried fruit, and fortified wholegrain cereals. Try to ensure that your toddler eats iron-rich foods daily.

Drinks

The best drink for your child in between meals is water. Avoid squash, fizzy drinks, juice drinks with added sugar and flavoured milks, which are often high in sugar, additives and sweeteners. If giving fruit juice, dilute it at least half and half with water. If your child has had diarrhoea, coconut water is a good drink, as it is rich in potassium, magnesium and calcium, making it an effective reydrating drink at times. It can also help prevent constipation.

FOODS TO AVOID

It is important to avoid giving the following foods to babies under 1 year old: lightly cooked eggs, honey, salted produce, processed meats and blue or unpasteurized cheese or dairy products.

No to Sugar

Both refined sugar and processed carbohydrates are devoid of nutrients and lead to blood sugar imbalances. For this reason, I've suggested in this book that you use xylitol. With a low glycemic index, xylitol has minimal impact on blood glucose levels and may help to maintain healthy teeth. If you cannot find xylitol, use raw cane sugar instead. Honey should not be given to children under one year old.

Be careful of foods and drinks labelled "sugar-free", as these will often contain aspartame and saccharin, which may adversely affect your child's behaviour.

Go Low with Salt

By focusing on whole and unprocessed foods, you will naturally reduce salt levels in your child's diet. Unfortunately, many processed foods, including those that are aimed at children, can be high in salt. These include foods such as breads, cereals, snack foods, biscuits and processed meats and cheese. Toddlers should consume only 2g salt (babies 1g).

Keep Your Child Chemical Free

Food colourings, flavourings, preservatives and pesticides can all adversely affect your child's health and behaviour. Many of the chemicals and E numbers found in processed foods are anti-nutrients – substances that interfere with our ability to absorb or to use essential nutrients and can also promote the loss of important nutrients from the body. Exposure to heavy metals can also be damaging, particularly to brain health. Try to reduce or avoid eating larger oily fish (see p.12) and avoid using aluminium or non-stick cookware.

CATERING FOR DIETS AND ALLERGIES

Allergies to certain foods, such as eggs, nuts, dairy, gluten and soya, are common, particularly in young children. Allergies can cause a diverse range of symptoms including fatigue, irritability, behavioural problems, hyperactivity and digestive upsets. Immune-system reactions can involve IgE antibodies resulting in an immediate, severe and potentially life-threatening reaction or more delayed IgG reactions, which can take anywhere from an hour to three days to show themselves. Food intolerances and sensitivities are reactions to food where there is no measurable antibody response. This can include lactose intolerance, where a child lacks the enzyme to digest milk sugar (lactose) and can develop diarrhoea and abdominal pain. The most common allergens are wheat and other gluten grains, milk, eggs, yeast-containing foods, shellfish, nuts, peanuts and soya.

The recipes in this book are clearly labelled for many of these key allergens, and many of the recipes are gluten free and dairy free. In addition, you can easily alter many of the recipes, for example using tamari soy sauce instead of standard soy sauce to make them gluten free. If you think your child is reacting to certain foods, it is worth seeking the advice of a qualified nutritionist to help with testing and devising an alternative nutrient-rich diet. Digestive problems are often the underlying factor in IgG allergies, so it is important to heal the gut with supplements as well as removing aggravating foods. Seek the support of a nutritional therapist.

If there is a family history of allergies (including eczema, asthma and hay fever), introduce new foods, particularly the common allergenic foods, one at a time and watch for any reaction.

Vegetarian Toddlers

A vegetarian diet for a toddler requires careful consideration and planning to ensure they receive all the nutrients they need to thrive. Certain nutrients can be low in vegetarian diets, including protein, essential fats, iron, zinc, calcium, iodine, vitamin B12 and vitamin D. Make sure you include plenty of nutrient-dense foods, such as dairy foods, avocados, eggs, ground nuts and seeds, nut and seed oils and nut butters (as long as there is no family history of allergies). Also, make sure that their diet is not too high in fibre-rich foods, which can upset their digestion and fill them up so that they do not receive adequate calories and energy.

SUPPLEMENTS

While a healthy diet is the foundation of optimum nutrition, surveys show that nutrient deficiencies in children are common.

Include a quality children's multivitamin and mineral formula in your child's diet as a useful insurance to keep your child physically and mentally healthy. Choose one free from added sugars, sweeteners, artificial flavours and colourings.

Many children are low in the essential omegas, so it is worth considering a supplement. Look for those that contain omega-3 fats DHA and EPA and the omega-6 fat GLA (gamma linolenic acid) found in evening primrose and borage oils.

In addition, you may wish to consider giving your toddler a probiotic, especially after a tummy bug, diarrhoea or being on a course of antibiotics. Probiotics are beneficial bacteria in the gut that maintain a healthy digestive system and support immune health.

SAFETY WITH FINGER FOODS

Whilst finger foods are a great way to encourage independent eating, there is a slight risk of choking. Do not give your child whole nuts, make sure he sits down to eat and do not leave him while eating. Teach him to chew and swallow before talking. Cut grapes and other fruits, meat, cheese and raw vegetables into small pieces that won't block airways.

Offer plenty of liquids when eating, but make sure liquids and solids are not swallowed at the same time.

VITAMIN / MINERAL	KEY FOOD SOURCES	SIGNS OF DEFICIENCY
B Vitamins Needed for energy production, important for function of the heart, nervous system	Whole grains, leafy green vegetables, eggs, meat, fish, pulses and beans	Low energy, depression, poor concentration and focus
Calcium Necessary for growth and maintenance of strong bones, teeth and cell walls, needed to regulate muscle contraction and heartbeat	Dairy products, nuts, seeds, leafy green vegetables, canned fish with bones, dried fruit, fortified milk alternatives	Anxiety, insomnia, poor bone and teeth health
Vitamin D Processed into a hormone via the liver and kidneys, it regulates calcium absorption – important for cell division and immune function	Main source is sunlight, oily fish, fortified dairy products, shiitake mushrooms and eggs.	Low immune function, depression, poor bone and teeth health
Zinc Vital component of many enzymes and necessary for energy production, wound healing and cell production	Seafood, nuts, seeds, natural yogurt, tahini, eggs, lean meats	Low immune function, poor appetite, loss of taste and smell, lack of concentration, slow wound healing
Iron Necessary for the production of haemoglobin in red blood cells and transporting oxygen around the body, needed for many of the body's enzymes	Leafy green vegetables, lean meats, eggs, pulses and beans, fortified cereals	Low energy, pallor, weakness, poor concentration, low immune function, depression, poor cognitive function, spoon-shaped nails or with ridges running lengthways
Magnesium Vital for the function of enzymes for energy production, cell metabolism, muscle and nerve function	Leafy green vegetables, nuts, seeds, beans	Irritability, anxiety, muscle cramps, low energy, poor bone and teeth health, depression, insomnia

BREAKFASTS

To get your child off to the best start in the day, breakfast is a must. Even if you feel rushed in the mornings or your child has a limited appetite, there are plenty of options in this chapter to suit the fussiest of eaters. If you provide them with a nourishing, low glycaemic breakfast, children will have more stable energy levels to help them concentrate through the morning. All the recipes in this chapter focus around slow-releasing carbohydrates, fibre, protein and essential fats to provide everything your child needs to make the most of their day ahead. Whether it is some Tropical Breakfast Bars or Cheesy Chilli Muffins, these finger foods are ideal to nourish the whole family – simple and fuss free, making it easy to experience a healthier start to the day.

cranberry seed bread

A delicious quick and easy sweet bread packed with omega-rich seeds and fibre. Using frozen cranberries keeps the bread lovely and moist.

MAKES 1 LOAF (10 SLICES)

PREPARATION + COOKING
15 + 40 minutes

STORAGE
Keep in the fridge for 2–3 days or freeze for up to 1 month.

SERVE THIS WITH...
Almond Chocolate Butter (see p.73) or pure fruit spread

HEALTH BENEFITS
Pumpkin seeds are nutrient-dense nuggets for children, providing plenty of protein, essential omega-3 and 6 fats as well as bone-supporting minerals manganese, magnesium, phosphorous and zinc. They are perfect for boosting flagging energy levels, being rich in protein and energy-giving nutrients iron, copper, zinc, magnesium and B vitamins.

light olive oil, for greasing
225g/8oz/1½ cups wholemeal self-raising flour
1 tsp bicarbonate of soda
2 tbsp pumpkin seeds
2 tbsp sunflower seeds
2 tbsp sesame seeds
5 eggs
90g/3¼oz/½ cup raw cane sugar or xylitol
finely grated zest of 1 orange
1 tbsp pure vanilla extract
5 tbsp olive oil or melted coconut oil
115g/4oz/1 cup frozen cranberries

1 Preheat the oven to 180°C/350°F/Gas 4. Lightly grease a 450g/1lb loaf tin with oil and line it with baking parchment.
2 Put the flour, bicarbonate of soda and seeds in a large bowl and stir well.
3 In another bowl, beat together the eggs, sugar, orange zest and vanilla extract until light and fluffy. Add the beaten mixture and the oil to the dry ingredients and mix well. Stir in the cranberries.
4 Pour the mixture into the prepared tin and bake for 35–40 minutes until golden brown and firm to the touch.
5 Leave to cool in the tin a little before turning out. Cut into slices to serve while still warm, or serve toasted.

carrot & raisin buns

These fibre-rich sweet buns resemble little carrot cakes, but are much healthier.

100ml/3½fl oz/scant ½ cup
   light olive oil, plus extra
   for greasing
3 eggs, beaten
115g/4oz/heaped ¾ cup
   wholemeal self-raising flour
115g/4oz/scant 1 cup self-
   raising flour

a pinch of cinnamon
2 carrots, peeled and
   finely grated
4 tbsp raisins
2 tbsp desiccated coconut
115g/4oz tinned crushed
   pineapple, drained

MAKES 10

PREPARATION + COOKING
15 + 20 minutes

STORAGE
Keep in the fridge for 2–3 days
or freeze for up to 1 month.

SERVE THIS WITH…
scrambled or boiled egg

HEALTH BENEFITS
Carrots are one of the richest sources of carotenoids: antioxidants known to promote healthy eyesight and protect the skin and eyes from UV damage. Carrots are easy to digest, even for babies, and, being rich in soluble fibre, help to promote healthy bowel function and regulate blood sugar levels.

1 Preheat the oven to 180°C/350°F/Gas 4. Lightly grease 10 holes in a mini-muffin tin with oil.

2 Beat together the oil and eggs to form a thick emulsion. Sift the flours into a bowl and add the cinnamon, carrots, raisins and coconut. Stir in the oil mixture and pineapple.

3 Spoon the mixture into the prepared muffin tin.

4 Bake for 20 minutes until firm and golden. Leave in the tin for 5 minutes, then turn out and cool on a wire rack.

date & spice muffins

These tasty muffins are gluten and dairy free.

MAKES 6

PREPARATION + COOKING
15 + 20 minutes

STORAGE
Keep in the fridge for 2–3 days or freeze for up to 1 month.

SERVE THIS WITH...
fresh fruit
yogurt smoothie

HEALTH BENEFITS
Cinnamon is a wonderful, warming spice known to help stabilize blood sugar levels by improving the uptake of glucose into the cells. It also lowers inflammation in the body and appears to possess antibacterial and antifungal properties, making it useful against bacterial and yeast infections.

4 tbsp light olive oil, plus extra for greasing
75g/2½oz/scant ½ cup almonds
60g/2¼oz/½ cup coconut flour
75g/2½oz/scant ⅔ cup gluten-free flour
½ tsp bicarbonate of soda
2 tsp gluten-free baking powder
a pinch of salt
1 tsp cinnamon
60g/2¼oz/½ cup finely chopped pitted dates

2 tbsp raw cane sugar or xylitol
2 bananas
4 eggs

CRUMBLE TOPPING
2 tbsp gluten-free porridge oats or buckwheat flakes
1 tbsp raw cane sugar or xylitol
1 tsp cinnamon
1 tbsp light olive oil

1 Preheat the oven to 180°C/350°F/Gas 4. Lightly grease a 6-hole muffin tin.

2 Pulse the topping ingredients in a food processor.

3 Put the almonds in a blender and blend to form a flour. Tip into a bowl with the both flours, bicarbonate of soda, baking powder, salt and cinnamon. Stir in the dates.

4 Blend together the oil, sugar, bananas and eggs. Pour into the almond mixture and beat for 5 minutes.

5 Spoon the mixture into the prepared muffin tin and sprinkle over the topping. Bake for 15–20 minutes until firm and golden. Leave to cool in the tins completely.

crunchy granola bites

Delicious crunchy oats, nuts and seeds are coated with a naturally sweet date paste and baked in the oven to form crisp nuggets.

light olive oil, for greasing
115g/4oz/scant 1¼ cups
    porridge oats
60g/2¼oz/⅔ cup flaked
    almonds
60g/2¼oz/½ cup chopped
    pecan nuts
15g/½oz/¼ cup flaked
    unsweetened coconut

60g/2¼oz/½ cup mixed dried
    berries
4 tbsp sunflower seeds
2 tbsp sesame seeds
½ tsp cinnamon
5 tbsp olive oil or melted
    coconut oil
60g/2¼oz/⅓ cup pitted dates
½ tsp pure vanilla extract

SERVES 6

PREPARATION + COOKING
10 + 45 minutes

STORAGE
Keep in an airtight container for
1–2 weeks.

SERVE THIS WITH...
fresh fruit

HEALTH BENEFITS
Oats are a perfect breakfast food for young children, providing plenty of slow-releasing carbohydrate and fibre to keep blood sugar levels even through the morning. They are a good source of the mineral magnesium, which is essential for energy production yet is often lacking in children's diet. Oats also provide selenium – an important antioxidant that protects the body from damage.

1 Preheat the oven to 150°C/300°F/Gas 2. Lightly grease a baking sheet with oil and line it with baking parchment.
2 Put the oats, nuts, coconut, berries, seeds and cinnamon in a large bowl and toss well.
3 Pour the olive oil into a blender. Add the dates and vanilla extract and process to form a sticky paste. Stir the mixture into the oats and mix thoroughly until everything is slightly sticky. Squeeze the mixture into little walnut-sized "nuggets" and space them out evenly over the prepared baking sheet.
4 Bake for 45 minutes or until golden brown. Leave to cool on the baking sheet.

tropical breakfast bars

HEALTH BENEFITS
If your child seems in low spirits and lethargic, cashew nuts may be the perfect food. Rich in copper and iron, cashew nuts can help to build red blood cells, which are essential for maintaining energy and brain function. They are also a useful source of the mineral magnesium (important for bone health) plus zinc to keep the immune system functioning optimally.

The delicious combination of pineapple and cashew nuts makes these the perfect "grab and go" healthy breakfast bars when time is short. Adding nut butter to the flour mixture greatly increases the protein and minerals in this bar and will help to satisfy even the hungriest of toddlers.

50ml/1¾fl oz/scant ¼ cup light
olive oil, plus extra for
greasing
175g/6oz/1½ cups dried
pineapple pieces, chopped
¼ ripe pineapple, diced
100g/3½oz cashew nut butter or
other nut butter

175g/6oz/1¾ cups porridge oats
175g/6oz/scant 1¼ cups
wholemeal self-raising flour
1 tsp baking powder
2 tbsp ground flaxseeds
2 tbsp sesame seeds
100g/3½oz/1 cup desiccated
coconut

MAKES 16

PREPARATION + COOKING
20 + 35 minutes

STORAGE
Keep in the fridge for 1 week
or freeze for up to 1 month.

SERVE THIS WITH...
fresh fruit

1 Preheat the oven to 180°C/350°F/Gas 4. Lightly grease a
25 x 30cm/10 x 12in shallow baking tin with oil and line it
with baking parchment.

2 Put the dried pineapple pieces in a bowl and cover with
boiling water. Leave for 15 minutes, then drain.

3 Put half of the dried pineapple into a blender with the
fresh pineapple, cashew nut butter and oil, and process to
form a thick purée.

4 Put the oats, flour and baking powder in a bowl. Stir in
the seeds, coconut and remaining dried pineapple. Pour
in the purée and mix thoroughly.

5 Spoon into the prepared tin and bake for 30–35 minutes
until golden brown. Cool in the tin, then cut into 16 slices.

raisin quinoa slices

Quinoa flakes are a nutrient-rich gluten-free addition to these bars and easy to digest, making them a perfect food for young children.

MAKES 12

PREPARATION + COOKING
15 + 40 minutes

STORAGE
Keep in the fridge for 2–3 days or slice and freeze for up to 1 month.

SERVE THIS WITH…
Greek yogurt
fresh fruit or a vegetable juice

HEALTH BENEFITS
Energizing and nutritious buckwheat is a delicious gluten-free grain particularly rich in magnesium – a critical mineral for supporting energy production in the body. It is a rich source of flavonoids, especially rutin, which are potent antioxidants shown to improve blood flow and circulation. It is a good source of fibre, too, helping to nourish the digestive system and keeping energy levels stable through the day.

light olive oil, for greasing
2 dessert apples, peeled and grated
60g/2¼oz/⅓ cup rice flour
60g/2¼oz/½ cup buckwheat flour
40g/1½oz/scant ½ cup quinoa flakes
2 tbsp raw cacao powder or 1 tbsp cocoa powder
½ tsp cinnamon
2 tsp gluten-free baking powder
1 tbsp ground flaxseeds
5 tbsp olive oil or melted coconut oil
2 tbsp raw cane sugar or xylitol
60g/2¼oz/½ cup raisins
2 tbsp mixed seeds, such as sunflower and sesame
2 eggs, beaten

1 Preheat the oven to 180°C/350°F/Gas 4. Lightly grease a 20cm/8in square baking tin with oil.
2 Put the apples, flours, quinoa flakes, cacao powder, cinnamon, baking powder and flaxseeds in a mixing bowl.
3 Heat the oil and the sugar in a small pan, add to the flour with the raisins, seeds and eggs and mix thoroughly.
4 Spoon the mixture into the prepared baking tin and bake for 40 minutes or until golden brown. Cut into bars while warm, then leave to cool in the tin.

berry blinis with sweet cherry sauce

These tasty pancakes are packed with protein.

125g/4½oz/heaped ¾ cup wholemeal self-raising flour
75g/2½oz/heaped ½ cup buckwheat flour
2 tsp baking powder
2 eggs, separated
190ml/6½fl oz/¾ cup semi-skimmed milk
200g/7oz ricotta cheese

75g/2½oz/¾ cup frozen mixed berries
1 tbsp olive oil or melted coconut oil

CHERRY SAUCE:
75g/2½oz fresh or thawed frozen pitted cherries
1 tbsp raw cane sugar or xylitol

1 To make the cherry sauce, put the cherries and sugar in a food processor and process to form a thick sauce.
2 Mix together the flours and baking powder in a bowl. Make a well in the centre, then gradually beat in the egg yolks, milk and ricotta. Beat thoroughly. Stir in the berries.
3 Whisk the egg whites until stiff. Stir a spoonful into the ricotta mixture to loosen, then fold in the rest.
4 Heat a little oil in a frying pan. Put 4 tablespoons of batter into the pan to form 4 little pancakes. Cook on one side for 2 minutes until little bubbles appear. Flip over and cook for 1 minute until golden. Cover while making 4 more.
5 Serve the pancakes with the cherry sauce drizzled over.

SERVES 4

PREPARATION + COOKING
15 + 14 minutes

STORAGE
Keep the pancakes in the fridge for 1–2 days and the sauce for 2–3 days.

SERVE THIS WITH...
toasted pistachio nuts
natural yogurt

HEALTH BENEFITS
Like all berries, cherries are exceptionally rich in antioxidants, especially anthocyanidins, which can help to prevent or repair cell damage from free radicals. These antioxidants can also help lower inflammation in the body, which may help with skin conditions such as eczema. Being a low glycaemic index fruit, they make an ideal snack for babies and toddlers to balance blood sugar levels through the morning.

almond & apricot scotch pancakes

These gluten-free pancakes are sweetened with apricots and use almonds instead of flour.

MAKES 12 (SERVES 4–6)

PREPARATION + COOKING
20 + 15 minutes + soaking + resting

STORAGE
Keep in the fridge for 1–2 days.

SERVE THIS WITH...
chopped pitted apricots
Greek yogurt

HEALTH BENEFITS
Toddlers can often have low iron levels, resulting in flagging energy levels, poor concentration and susceptibility to infections. Dried apricots are a useful vegetarian source of iron, providing 6.3mg iron per 100g. They are also a concentrated source of other minerals, including potassium, as well as bone-friendly nutrients calcium, magnesium and beta-carotene.

30g/1oz/scant ¼ cup ready-to-eat dried apricots, chopped
juice of 1 orange
200g/7oz/1¼ cups almonds
2 eggs
1 tbsp light olive oil
2 tsp pure vanilla extract
½ tsp bicarbonate of soda
1 tsp gluten-free baking powder
2 tbsp olive oil

1 Soak the apricots in the juice for 10 minutes to soften.
2 Put the almonds in a blender and blend to form a flour. Tip into a bowl and set aside.
3 Put the apricots and juice, eggs, oil and vanilla extract in the blender and process until smooth. Add the almond flour, bicarbonate of soda and baking powder and blend to form a smooth batter. Leave to rest for 10 minutes.
4 Heat a little oil in a large frying pan. Put 4 large spoonfuls of the batter into the pan to make 4 pancakes. Cook for 2–3 minutes until bubbles form on the surface. Flip the pancakes over carefully and cook for a further 2 minutes until golden. Remove from the pan and cover to keep warm. Repeat with the remaining batter until you have made 12 pancakes. Serve straightaway.

apple-cinnamon french toast

Give French toast a fruity twist with these delicious bite-sized toasted sandwiches. Choose wholemeal bread for slow-releasing carbohydrates and additional fibre.

2 dessert apples, peeled, cored and chopped
1 tsp cinnamon
4 slices of wholemeal bread

2 eggs
4 tbsp semi-skimmed milk
1 tbsp olive oil or melted coconut oil

1 Put the apples in a small pan with 2 tablespoons water. Cover and simmer for 10 minutes until soft. Purée with a stick blender or press through a sieve. Leave to cool. Stir in half of the cinnamon.

2 Spread 2 slices of the bread with the apple purée. Put the other slices on top to form 2 sandwiches.

3 Put the eggs, milk and remaining cinnamon in a bowl and whisk well. Heat the oil in a large frying pan.

4 Carefully dip the sandwiches into the egg mixture and coat all over. Put the sandwiches in the pan and fry gently for 3–4 minutes on each side until golden.

5 Remove from the pan and leave to cool slightly. Serve cut into quarters on the diagonal.

SERVES 4

PREPARATION + COOKING
15 + 14 minutes

STORAGE
Best eaten immediately.

SERVE THIS WITH…
Greek or natural yogurt

HEALTH BENEFITS
Apples contain plant compounds called polyphenols, which have been shown to support immune health and lower inflammation in the body. Being rich in soluble fibre and pectin, they are particularly useful for tackling tummy troubles and improving bowel health. Keeping the skin on some of the apples will provide additional fibre and nutrients.

chocolate peanut waffles

MAKES 8

PREPARATION + COOKING
15 + 10 minutes

STORAGE
Keep in the fridge for 1 day.

SERVE THIS WITH...
fresh fruit
yogurt
Sweet Cherry Sauce
  (see page 29)

HEALTH BENEFITS
Chocolate can be a healthy
food as long as you use it in its
unsweetened, low-processed
form. Dark chocolate, raw
chocolate, cocoa and raw cacao
powder are rich in flavonoids
– powerful antioxidants known
to help protect the body from
damage. They also contain
brain-stimulating chemicals such
as theobromine, tyramine and
phenylethylamine, which can lift
mood and boost brain function.

Quick and easy to make and packed with
energizing protein and slow-releasing carbs, this
sensational breakfast treat will be a firm family
favourite. The waffles are delicious served with
fresh fruit and yogurt, but are also wonderful
served plain as a snack at any time of day.

115g/4oz/¾ cup wholemeal
  self-raising flour
75g/2½oz/scant ⅔ cup plain
  flour
1 tsp baking powder
2 tbsp cocoa powder
2 eggs

3 tbsp wholegrain peanut butter
2 tbsp raw cane sugar or xylitol
1 tbsp light olive oil, plus extra
  for greasing
200ml/7fl oz/generous ¾ cup
  full-fat or semi-skimmed
  milk

1 Sift the flours, baking powder and cocoa powder into a
food processor, tipping in the bran from the sieve.
2 Put the eggs, peanut butter, sugar and oil in a bowl and
whisk to combine. Add to the processor and process with
enough of the milk to form a thick batter.
3 Grease a 4-hole waffle iron with oil and ladle the batter
on to the waffle iron according to the manufacturer's
instructions. Cook for 4–5 minutes until golden and crisp.
Repeat with the remaining batter. (Note that if you have
only a 2-hole iron, the cooking will take twice as long.)
4 Serve hot or cold.

fruity popovers

Children love these fruit-filled popovers.

100g/3½oz/heaped ¾ cup
   plain flour, sifted
1 tbsp ground flaxseeds
2 tbsp raw cane sugar or xylitol
4 eggs

300ml/10½fl oz/scant 1¼ cups
   full-fat or semi-skimmed milk
2 ripe pears, peeled, cored
   and diced
1 large handful of blueberries
1 tbsp olive oil

1 Put the flour, flaxseeds and sugar in a bowl. Whisk in the eggs, then pour in the milk slowly while whisking to avoid lumps. Cover the batter with clear film and leave overnight in the fridge.

2 Preheat the oven to 220°C/425°F/Gas 7. Spoon the fruit into the batter mixture and stir to combine.

3 Put a little of the oil into 4 holes in a muffin tin and heat in the oven until hot (about 5 minutes). Remove from the oven and quickly fill the tins with the fruit batter.

4 Cook for 20–25 minutes until puffed and golden brown.

5 Leave to cool slightly before serving.

SERVES 4

PREPARATION + COOKING
10 + 25 minutes + chilling

STORAGE
Keep in the fridge for 1 day.

SERVE THIS WITH...
poached or fresh berries
natural yogurt

HEALTH BENEFITS
To keep energy levels high in the morning, opt for fruits with a low glycaemic index, such as pears. A good source of soluble fibre, they are also a low-allergen fruit, making them a perfect choice for young children. Pears are also a good source of potassium, to help balance fluid levels, rehydrate the body following bouts of diarrhoea and prevent muscle cramp. Flaxseeds will increase the fibre content and omega-3 fats, too.

vegetable rostis with herby cottage cheese

Topped with a delicious herby cheese, these make a sensational breakfast that will be enjoyed by babies and toddlers alike.

SERVES 4

PREPARATION + COOKING
15 + 10 minutes

STORAGE
Keep in the fridge for 2 days.

SERVE THIS WITH...
low-sugar baked beans
grilled tomatoes

HEALTH BENEFITS
Parsley is an incredibly nutritious herb, rich in iron and vitamin C, making it a wonderful energizing food for young children. Packed with antioxidants, known as flavonoids, and beta-carotene, parsley provides protection to cells, helps lower inflammation and supports immune health. It is also thought to be a diuretic, assisting kidney function and reducing fluid retention.

1 small baking potato
1 parsnip, peeled and grated
1 shallot, grated
25g/1oz butter
2 tbsp olive oil or melted coconut oil

115g/4oz full-fat cottage cheese
1 tbsp chopped parsley
1 tbsp capers, rinsed and drained
freshly ground black pepper

1 Coarsely grate the potato on to a clean tea towel and squeeze out the excess moisture. Tip into a bowl and add the parsnip and shallot. Melt the butter in a small pan and stir into the mixture. Season with pepper.

2 Heat the oil in a frying pan. Shape the mixture into 4 patties and put in the pan. Press down with a spatula and cook for 5 minutes on each side until golden and crisp.

3 Mix together the cottage cheese, parsley and capers. Season with a little black pepper.

4 Transfer the rostis to plates and top each one with a little of the herby cheese to serve.

mexican sweetcorn fritters

These lightly spiced fritters are delicious hot or cold served with a little chilli or tomato sauce. For a more substantial brunch dish, accompany with some ham or eggs. An easy way to introduce children to new flavours and spices.

3 tbsp polenta
60g/2¼oz/½ cup plain flour
a pinch of salt
4 tsp baking powder
15g/½oz butter
1 egg, beaten
5 tbsp milk
½ tsp dried chilli flakes
a pinch of smoked paprika
1 tbsp chopped coriander leaves
125g/4½oz/heaped ¾ cup frozen sweetcorn kernels, thawed
3 tbsp olive oil or melted coconut oil

1 Mix the polenta, flour, salt and baking powder in a bowl.
2 Melt the butter in a small pan, then add to the bowl with the egg and milk and whisk to form a batter. Add the chilli flakes, paprika and coriander, then stir in the corn.
3 Heat the oil in a frying pan and add 4 tablespoonfuls of the mixture to the pan to form 4 little fritters. Cook for 2–3 minutes on each side until browned. Remove from the pan and repeat twice with the mixture to make 12 in total.

SERVES 4

PREPARATION + COOKING
15 + 18 minutes

STORAGE
Keep in the fridge for 1 day.

SERVE THIS WITH...
lean ham or high-quality meat sausages

HEALTH BENEFITS
Sweetcorn is packed full of brain-boosting and energizing B vitamins, including thiamine (B1), pantothenic acid (B5) and folate. Thiamin is critical for cognitive function, as it is needed for the synthesis of acetylcholine, a neurotransmitter essential for memory. Sweetcorn is also a great source of energizing magnesium, manganese and immune-supporting vitamin C.

avocado bagel melts

These delicious quick bites use wholegrain or seeded bagels to help sustain energy levels through the morning. Topped with mozzarella for protein, plus nutrient-dense avocado, this is a super-healthy fast-food option.

HEALTH BENEFITS
Nutrient-dense avocados are the perfect food for young children, being rich in monounsaturated fat, which is easily digested, plus energizing B vitamins. A good source of protective antioxidants, including vitamins A, C and E, avocados are a great food for maintaining healthy skin.

2 tbsp sun-dried tomato pesto
2 wholegrain or seeded bagels,
    split in half horizontally
2 tbsp mayonnaise

1 small ripe avocado, halved,
    pitted and diced
2 plum tomatoes, diced
60g/2¼oz mozzarella cheese,
    grated

SERVES 4

PREPARATION + COOKING
10 + 5 minutes

STORAGE
Best eaten immediately.

SERVE THIS WITH...
1 handful of spinach

1 Preheat the grill to high.

2 Spread the tomato pesto over the cut sides of the bagels.

3 Mix together the mayonnaise, avocado and tomatoes in a bowl. Spoon the mixture on top of each bagel and sprinkle with the grated cheese.

4 Put under the grill for about 5 minutes until the cheese melts. Serve warm.

omelette roll-ups

These little rolls are filled with flakes of hot-smoked salmon and cream cheese, making this an incredibly energizing and brain-boosting dish.

SERVES 4

PREPARATION + COOKING
10 + 8 minutes

STORAGE
Keep in the fridge for 1 day.

SERVE THIS WITH...
grilled tomatoes
grilled mushrooms

HEALTH BENEFITS
Eggs really are the perfect breakfast food to start your child's day. A complete source of high-quality protein, plus energizing B vitamins, selenium, iodine, vitamin D and iron. They are also rich in the nutrient choline, used by the body to produce the neurotransmitter acetylcholine, involved in cognitive function and memory.

4 eggs
1 tbsp olive oil or melted coconut oil
60g/2¼oz hot-smoked salmon
1 tbsp chopped dill
4 tbsp cream cheese
freshly ground black pepper

1 Beat the eggs in a bowl and season with black pepper.
2 Heat half the oil in an omelette pan and pour in half of the beaten eggs. Swirl the eggs around the pan and cook for a few seconds until the bottom of the omelette is lightly set. Push the set parts of the omelette into the uncooked centre of the omelette and cook again until the omelette is set and lightly golden underneath.
3 Flip the omelette over and brown lightly for a few seconds. Turn out onto a chopping board. Repeat with the remaining eggs to make a second omelette.
4 Flake the salmon and mix together in bowl with the dill and cream cheese. Season with a little black pepper. Spread the mixture on one side of each omelette, leaving a gap at the edges.
5 Roll up each omelette tightly and cut into slices. Serve warm or cold.

cheesy-chilli muffins

A spicy savoury option for breakfast. You can vary the amount of chilli sauce you use to suit your child.

light olive oil, for greasing
150g/5½oz/1¼ cups self-raising flour
150g/5½oz/1 cup wholemeal self-raising flour
2 tbsp sweet chilli sauce
2 eggs, beaten
250ml/9fl oz/1 cup buttermilk

75g/2½oz butter
125g/4½oz Cheddar cheese: 50g/1¾oz grated and the rest cut into little cubes
150g/5½oz/1 cup frozen sweetcorn, thawed
1 plum tomato, diced

1 Preheat the oven to 200°C/400°F/Gas 6. Lightly grease 10 holes in a muffin tin with oil.

2 Mix the flours together in a bowl.

3 Beat together the sweet chilli sauce, eggs and buttermilk. Melt the butter in a small pan and add to the mixture. Stir the batter into the flour with half the grated cheese and the sweetcorn and tomato.

4 Spoon 1 tablespoon of the mixture into each muffin hole. Put a cube of cheese in the centre, cover with more mixture and sprinkle over the remaining grated cheese.

5 Bake for 20 minutes until the muffins are golden and have risen. Turn out onto a wire rack to cool slightly. Serve warm.

MAKES 10

PREPARATION + COOKING
15 + 20 minutes

STORAGE
Keep in the fridge for 2 days or freeze for up to 1 month.

SERVE THIS WITH...
low-sugar baked beans
grilled mushrooms

HEALTH BENEFITS
Chillies not only give a wonderful spicy heat to foods but are also rich in antioxidant vitamins A (beta-carotene), C and E as well as folic acid and potassium. Great for stimulating circulation, they also have mild analgesic properties that may be useful in helping to ease headaches and also sinusitis.

LUNCHES

Keep your child focused and alert all afternoon with a nutritious, satisfying lunch. Whether you are looking for packed lunch ideas beyond the humble sandwich or finger foods straight from the oven, in this chapter you will find a whole range of delicious and nourishing dishes to enjoy. Designed with busy parents in mind, they can be prepared in advance, and, being finger foods, are perfect for days out. Many of the recipes are ideal for picnics, brunches and parties, too. Whether you are rushing around or have a little more time to spare, by providing your children with a nourishing lunch, you can boost their energy levels, helping them to make the most of their day.

peanut chicken bites

These are moist, crispy and incredibly healthy.

SERVES 4

PREPARATION + COOKING
20 + 30 minutes + chilling

STORAGE
Keep in the fridge for 2 days.

SERVE THIS WITH...
Raita (see page 58)
steamed vegetables
sweet potato wedges, baked in
   olive oil
Peaches with Berry Syrup
   (see page 128)

HEALTH BENEFITS
Garlic is a wonderful protective
food for children: being a
natural antibiotic, it can help to
protect from bacterial and fungal
infections. A useful decongestant
and immune-supporting spice,
it is a great choice for relieving
symptoms of coughs and colds.
Rich in sulphurous compounds,
it helps to stimulate liver
detoxification. In addition, it is
beneficial for skin conditions
such as eczema.

3 tbsp Greek yogurt
1 tbsp lemon juice
1 garlic clove, crushed
½ tsp cumin
½ tsp garam masala or mango
   powder

4 skinless, boneless chicken
   thighs, cut in half
175g/6oz/heaped 1 cup roasted
   unsalted peanuts
4 tbsp desiccated coconut
light olive oil, for greasing

1 Put the yogurt, lemon juice, garlic, cumin and garam
masala in a bowl and whisk to combine. Add the chicken
thighs, toss to coat in the mixture, then cover and leave
to marinate in the fridge for 30 minutes.

2 Put the peanuts in a food processor and process into
coarse crumbs. Tip on to a plate and mix with the coconut.

3 Preheat the oven to 200°C/400°F/Gas 6. Lightly grease
a baking sheet with oil and line it with baking parchment.

4 Coat the chicken thighs completely in the peanut
mixture and put on the prepared baking sheet. Bake for
20–30 minutes until golden brown and cooked through.

chicken & veg pastries

These little pastries are healthy and portable.

1 tbsp olive oil, plus extra for
   greasing
½ red onion, finely chopped
1 garlic clove, crushed
175g/6oz lean chicken mince
100g/3½oz broccoli florets,
   finely chopped
1 tbsp tomato purée
125g/4½oz tinned sweetcorn

1 egg, beaten
freshly ground black pepper

PASTRY
175g/6oz/scant 1½ cups plain
   flour, plus extra for dusting
1 tbsp ground flaxseeds
75g/2½oz chilled unsalted
   butter, diced

SERVES 4

PREPARATION + COOKING
20 + 25 minutes + chilling

STORAGE
Keep in the fridge for 2 days.

SERVE THIS WITH...
coleslaw
mixed salad
Mango Fruit Lollies
  (see page 124)

HEALTH BENEFITS
Cruciferous vegetables, such
as broccoli, are superfoods for
your children. They are packed
with powerful phytonutrient
antioxidants, such as
sulphoraphane and indoles, as
well as beta-carotene, which can
help protect against cell damage,
support liver function and
promote a healthy respiratory
tract and skin. Broccoli is also
a good source of folic acid and
iron, which are important for
haemoglobin production and
healthy red blood cells.

1 To make the pastry, sift the flour and flaxseeds together
in a large bowl. Rub in the butter until you have a soft
crumb texture. Add cold water to form a firm dough. Shape
into a ball, cover with clear film and chill for 30 minutes.
2 Heat the oil in a frying pan and sauté the onion and garlic.
Add the chicken, and brown. Add the broccoli, purée and
corn and season with pepper. Stir for 2 minutes, then cool.
3 Preheat the oven to 200°C/400°F/Gas 6. Roll out the
pastry. Stamp out 8 rounds with a 10cm/4in cutter. Put
a spoonful of mixture in the centre of each round. Brush
the edge with water and fold the pastry over the filling.
Seal the pastries by pinching the edges together.
4 Put the pastries on an oiled baking sheet and brush
with beaten egg. Bake for 20–25 minutes until browned.

tandoori chicken strips

Lightly spiced strips of tender chicken breast.

SERVES 4

PREPARATION + COOKING
20 + 20 minutes + chilling

STORAGE
Keep in the fridge for 1 day.

SERVE THIS WITH...
strips of naan bread
Raita (see page 58)
wilted spinach
homemade dahl
Coconut Jelly Squares
  (see page 127)

HEALTH BENEFITS
Yogurt is a good protein food, rich in amino acids such as tyrosine to boost alertness, mood and concentration. Plain yogurt is also a useful source of calcium plus healthy bacteria known to help promote healthy digestion, immune health and absorption of nutrients.

250g/9oz skinless, boneless
  chicken breast fillets
1 tsp chaat masala spice mix
1 tsp lemon juice

MARINADE
250g/9oz/1 cup plain yogurt

1 tsp garam masala
½ tsp red chilli powder
a pinch of salt
2 tbsp lemon juice
1 garlic clove
2cm/¾in piece root ginger,
  peeled

1 Put all the ingredients for the marinade in a mini-chopper or blender and process until smooth.
2 Score the chicken breasts lightly with a sharp knife and put in a lidded container. Pour the marinade over the chicken and rub in well. Leave in the fridge for at least 20 minutes or overnight.
3 Preheat the oven to 200°C/400°F/Gas 6. Put the chicken on a non-stick baking sheet and cook for 5 minutes. Reduce the heat to 180°C/350°F/Gas 4 and cook for a further 10–15 minutes until the chicken is golden and cooked through (the juices should run clear when it is pierced in the thickest part with a skewer).
4 Remove from the oven and leave to rest for 5 minutes. Sprinkle with the chaat masala and lemon juice. Slice the chicken into strips.

chicken yakitori sticks

A sensational Asian-style chicken dish.

250g/9oz chicken breast fillets,
   cut into thin strips
4 tbsp mirin
2 tbsp kecap manis
2 tsp reduced-salt soy sauce
1 tbsp lemon juice and finely
   grated zest of 1 lemon
3 tbsp rice wine vinegar
2 tbsp raw cane sugar or xylitol
1 tsp toasted sesame seeds

1 Put the chicken in a shallow dish. Combine the mirin, kecap manis and soy sauce together in a jug and pour the mixture over the chicken. Leave in the fridge to marinate for 2–3 hours or overnight. Meanwhile, soak 8 mini wooden skewers in water for 30 minutes.
2 Thread the chicken strips onto the skewers, reserving the marinade.
3 Preheat the grill to high. Cook the chicken for 7–8 minutes, turning frequently, until the chicken is cooked through (the juices should run clear when it is pierced in the thickest part with a skewer).
4 Meanwhile, pour the reserved marinade into a small pan. Add the lemon juice, zest, vinegar and sugar and bring to the boil. Simmer for 5 minutes until syrupy. Stir in the sesame seeds and pour into a small bowl. Leave to cool.
5 Remove the skewers. Serve with the dipping sauce.

SERVES 4

PREPARATION + COOKING
15 + 13 minutes + chilling

STORAGE
Keep in the fridge for 1 day.

SERVE THIS WITH…
stir-fried vegetables
rice noodles
Frozen Pineapple Cheesecake
  Slice (see page 138)

HEALTH BENEFITS
Sesame seeds are a good source of calcium and magnesium, plus B vitamins, which can help to calm your child and aid relaxation of nerve and muscle cells. They are also rich in immune-supporting zinc, antioxidant vitamin E and omega-6 fatty acids, which are beneficial for healthy skin.

duck lettuce wraps

Healthy and delicious protein-rich wraps.

2 duck breasts
1 tbsp reduced-salt soy sauce
2 tsp honey or agave nectar
4 large romaine lettuce leaves
1 tbsp toasted sesame seeds

CHUTNEY
5 tbsp raw cane sugar or xylitol
1 star anise
½ tsp cinnamon
115g/4oz/¾ cup dried
   cranberries
200g/7oz/2 cups frozen
   cranberries
juice of 1 orange

1 Preheat the oven to 200°C/400°F/Gas 6.
2 Remove any fat from the duck. Mix together the soy sauce and honey and rub over the duck. Heat a dry frying pan and sear the duck for 2 minutes on each side. Transfer to a dish and roast in the oven for 12–15 minutes until cooked through. Leave to cool, then slice into strips.
3 To make the chutney, put the sugar, spices and 4 tablespoons water in a pan and bring to the boil. Add the cranberries and juice and simmer for 5–6 minutes, mashing down the fruit to form a soft purée. Leave to cool.
4 To assemble, put a few slices of duck in the centre of a lettuce leaf. Spoon over a little chutney and sesame seeds. Fold the lettuce leaf over the filling and roll up, folding in the sides as you roll to form a wrap.

SERVES 6

PREPARATION + COOKING
20 + 20 minutes

STORAGE
Keep the duck in the fridge for 1 day and the chutney for 4 days.

SERVE THIS WITH…
cucumber and red pepper sticks
Chunky Breadsticks (see page 87)
Summer Berry Ice Cups
   (see page 125)

HEALTH BENEFITS
Duck breast is an excellent source of lean protein, containing all the essential amino acids needed for growing children. It is also packed with iron, zinc and B vitamins, required for energy production and keeping your child alert and focused. Duck is a good source of selenium: an important mineral for a healthy immune system, thyroid function and a potent antioxidant for protecting cells, including brain cells, from damage.

pork & apple burgers

Lean pork mince with grated apple create simple moist burgers that are packed with flavour. Babies and older children love them.

light olive oil, for drizzling and
    greasing
250g/9oz lean pork mince
1 shallot, finely chopped
1 garlic clove, crushed

1 tbsp chopped coriander
1 dessert apple, peeled, cored
    and grated
2 tsp cornflour

1 Preheat the oven to 200°C/400°F/Gas 6. Lightly grease a baking sheet with oil and line it with baking parchment.
2 Put all the ingredients in a large bowl and mix well. With lightly oiled hands, shape the mixture into 8 small round burgers. Put on the prepared baking sheet and drizzle with a little olive oil.
3 Bake for 20–25 minutes, turning over halfway through so that they are golden brown all over.
4 To serve, put a burger in a lettuce leaf and top with a little tomato sauce.

SERVES 4

PREPARATION + COOKING
20 + 25 minutes

STORAGE
Keep in the fridge for 2 days.

SERVE THIS WITH...
little gem lettuce leaves
sliced tomatoes
Tomato Chutney (see page 105)
coleslaw
mixed salad
fresh fruit salad

HEALTH BENEFITS
Coriander is a versatile herb, in that both the leaves and seeds can be used in dishes. Known for its anti-bacterial properties, it is effective in protecting against bacterial infections, promoting digestion and relieving intestinal gas and stomach upsets. Being rich in antioxidants, it also has beneficial anti-inflammatory properties.

023

baked ham & egg cups

Eggs baked in a basket of lean ham and topped with tomato creates a fun hand-sized quiche – but without the pastry.

SERVES 4

PREPARATION + COOKING
10 + 8 minutes

STORAGE
Keep in the fridge for 1 day.

SERVE THIS WITH…
mixed salad
Squash Scones (see page 82)
fresh fruit

HEALTH BENEFITS
When choosing ham, choose cuts from the deli made from 100% pork, without colours, additives or fillers. Ideally, make sure it is organic. For small children, it is important to watch the sodium content, so aim for meats with less than 0.25g sodium per 100g. There are also some excellent nitrate-free meats available.

light olive oil, for greasing
4 slices of lean ham
2 tomatoes, finely chopped
Tabasco sauce (optional)

4 eggs
60g/2¼oz Cheddar cheese, grated
freshly ground black pepper

1 Preheat the oven to 200°C/400°F/Gas 6.

2 Lightly grease 4 holes in a muffin tin with oil. Put a slice of ham in each hole so that it covers the base and sides completely and sticks out of the top.

3 Divide the tomatoes between the holes and season with a dash of Tabasco, if using. Carefully crack an egg into the centre of each hole. Season with black pepper, then sprinkle over the grated cheese.

4 Bake for 5–8 minutes until the eggs are just set and the cheese has melted. Cool slightly, then remove from the tin.

toads in the holes

Crispy and golden little toads in the holes are perfect for children on the go.

1 tbsp light olive oil, plus extra
    for greasing
4 pork sausages (at least 85%
    meat content)
1 shallot, chopped
60g/2¼oz/½ cup plain flour

150ml/5fl oz/scant ⅔ cup
    semi-skimmed milk
1 egg, beaten
2 tsp Dijon mustard
1 tsp chopped thyme
freshly ground black pepper

1 Preheat the oven to 200°C/400°F/Gas 6.

2 Lightly grease 4 holes in a large muffin tin with oil.

3 Heat the oil in a frying pan and fry the sausages for about 5 minutes until golden brown and cooked through. One minute before the end of the cooking time, add the shallot and sauté until soft. Leave the sausages to cool a little, then cut into chunks. Put in a bowl with the shallot.

4 Put the flour, milk, egg and mustard in a blender and process to form a smooth batter. Season with a little black pepper and stir in the thyme.

5 Put the prepared tin in the oven and heat for 2–3 minutes until hot. Remove from the oven and divide the sausage mixture between the holes. Pour in the batter and return to the oven. Bake for 20 minutes until risen and golden brown. Leave to cool slightly before serving.

SERVES 4

PREPARATION + COOKING
15 + 25 minutes

STORAGE
Keep in the fridge for 1 day.

SERVE THIS WITH...
low-sugar baked beans
steamed vegetables
Lemon Cheesecake
    (see page 133)
fresh berries

HEALTH BENEFITS
Sausages can be a relatively healthy option if you choose those with a high meat content, preferably around 85% meat, using free-range or organic meat. As they are already seasoned, avoid using additional salt – instead flavour with herbs and spices to provide extra flavour.

lamb-stuffed peppers

SERVES 4

PREPARATION + COOKING
20 + 30 minutes

STORAGE
Keep in the fridge for 2 days.

SERVE THIS WITH...
sweet potato wedges baked
  in a little olive oil
mixed salad
fresh fruit
natural yogurt

HEALTH BENEFITS
The healthy monounsaturated
fats in olives, together with their
phenol content, make them
wonderfully protective foods
useful for reducing inflammation,
which can be helpful for
conditions such as asthma and
eczema. Packed with healthy
fats, they help to slow down the
rate of release of glucose into the
bloodstream, helping to balance
energy levels through the day.

This Spanish-inspired dish uses pepper halves
as shells for the tangy lamb and olive filling.

1 tbsp olive or melted cocoonut
  oil, plus extra for greasing
1 shallot, finely chopped
2 garlic cloves, crushed
175g/6oz lamb mince
½ tsp cumin
a pinch of chilli flakes

a pinch of ground cloves
8 pitted black olives, chopped
1 tbsp pine nuts
4 tbsp passata
2 red peppers, halved and
  deseeded
freshly ground black pepper

1 Preheat the oven to 200°C/400°F/Gas 6. Lightly grease
a baking sheet with oil.
2 Heat the oil in a large frying pan and sauté the shallot and
garlic for 2 minutes until soft. Add the lamb and spices
and stir for about 10 minutes, until the lamb is cooked
through, then stir in the olives, pine nuts and passata.
3 Put the pepper halves in a pan of boiling water and
blanch for 2–3 minutes to soften slightly. Drain and dry
on kitchen paper.
4 Put the pepper halves on the prepared baking sheet. Fill
with the lamb mixture and season with black pepper.
5 Bake for 15 minutes until the peppers are lightly golden
around the edges. Leave to cool slightly before serving.

baked spring rolls

These are much healthier than the fried version.

1 tsp cornflour
2 tsp rice wine vinegar
2 tsp reduced-salt soy sauce
1 egg white, beaten
200g/7oz lean lamb fillet,
    sliced into thin strips
1 tbsp light olive oil, plus extra
    for greasing and brushing

2cm/¾in piece root ginger,
    peeled and grated
1 garlic clove, crushed
250g/9oz mixed stir-fry
    vegetables
2 tbsp sweet chilli sauce
8 filo pastry sheets, cut in half
    to make 16 squares

1 Preheat the oven to 220°C/425°F/Gas 7. Lightly grease a baking sheet with oil.

2 Mix the cornflour, vinegar, soy sauce and egg white with enough water to form a paste. Toss the lamb in it.

3 Heat the oil in a frying pan and sauté the ginger, garlic and lamb for 3–4 minutes until the meat starts to brown. Add the vegetables, sweet chilli sauce and a little water if too dry. Fry until the lamb is cooked. Leave to cool.

4 Lay a square of filo with one point facing you, brush with oil, then put another piece on top. Put 1 teaspoon of the mixture in the centre of the pastry. Roll up, folding in the sides as you roll. Repeat to form 8 rolls.

5 Put seam side down on the baking sheet. Brush with oil. Bake for 15–20 minutes until golden and crisp. Serve.

SERVES 8

PREPARATION + COOKING
20 + 30 minutes

STORAGE
Keep in the fridge for 2 days.

SERVE THIS WITH...
cucumber and red pepper sticks
Tomato Chutney (see page 105)
Griddled Pineapple
  (see page 130)
natural yogurt

HEALTH BENEFITS
Ginger is a well-known digestive aid and a useful remedy for nausea as well as indigestion and stomach upsets. If your child suffers with sinus problems or frequent coughs and colds, including root ginger in their diet can stimulate circulation and help expel phlegm. Rich in powerful plant phytonutrients known as gingerols, it also has anti-inflammatory action and may help to alleviate conditions such as asthma and sinusitis.

027

steak gremolata rolls

This simple dish, packed with protein and energizing lean beef, is great for when your child's energy levels are low.

SERVES 4

PREPARATION + COOKING
15 + 10 minutes

STORAGE
Keep in the fridge for 1 day.

SERVE THIS WITH...
shredded lettuce
sliced tomatoes
coleslaw
Frozen Blueberry & Chocolate
Slice (see page 135)

HEALTH BENEFITS
Lean beef is a good source of protein, energizing B vitamins and iron. B vitamins are also essential for the production of neurotransmitters, which are essential for brain function and memory. Beef also provides plenty of zinc, which is often low in children and an important mineral for wound healing and immune support.

finely grated zest of 1 lemon
1 garlic clove, crushed
1 small handful of flat-leaf
   parsley, finely chopped
2 tbsp light olive oil

2 minute steaks, about
   100g/3½oz each
8 cherry tomatoes, quartered
4 wholemeal rolls

1 Put the lemon, garlic and parsley and 1 tablespoon of the oil in a bowl and mix well.

2 Heat the remaining oil in a large frying pan. Put the steaks in the pan and cook on both sides until brown and cooked through, about 3–4 minutes on each side. Just before the end of the cooking time, add the tomatoes to the pan and cook briefly to soften.

3 Remove the steaks from the pan and sprinkle over half the parsley mixture. Leave the steaks to rest for 5 minutes, then slice each steak thinly.

4 Cut the rolls in half and toast the cut sides lightly.

5 Put a little shredded lettuce on the bottom halves of the rolls, then put the steak slices and tomatoes on top. Sprinkle over the remaining parsley mixture and put the toasted tops of the rolls on top.

tostada chilli wedges

Corn tortillas filled with beef and refried beans.

1 tbsp olive oil, plus extra for
   brushing
1 small red onion, finely
   chopped
1 red chilli, deseeded and
   finely chopped
2 garlic cloves, crushed
175g/6oz lean beef mince

400g/14oz tinned kidney beans,
   drained and rinsed
½ tsp low-salt vegetable
   bouillon powder
1 tomato, chopped
4 corn tortillas
60g/2¼oz Cheddar cheese,
   grated

1 Heat the oil in a frying pan, add the onion, chilli and
garlic and sauté for 2 minutes. Add the mince and continue
to cook for 6–8 minutes until the beef turns brown.
2 Add the beans and cook, uncovered, for 2–3 minutes
until hot. Use a potato masher to break up the beans.
3 Dissolve the vegetable bouillon in 4 tablespoons of
boiling water. Add the stock and tomato and continue to
cook for about 5 minutes until the beef is cooked.
4 Put 2 tortillas on a baking sheet and spoon over the
mixture. Sprinkle with the cheese, put the other tortillas
on top and press down lightly. Brush the top with oil.
5 Preheat the grill to high. Toast the tortillas for 5 minutes
until the cheese has melted and the top is golden. Cut into
wedges to serve.

SERVES 4

PREPARATION + COOKING
15 + 25 minutes

STORAGE
Keep in the fridge for 1 day.

SERVE THIS WITH...
mixed salad
Raita (see page 58)
Mango Fruit Lollies
   (see page 124)

HEALTH BENEFITS
Kidney beans are a great
vegetarian source of protein.
They are rich in folate and iron,
both of which are important for
maintaining energy levels and
the production of the immune
system's antibodies and white
blood cells. Beans also contain
high levels of fibre, which help
ensure a healthy digestion and
alleviate constipation.

fruity salmon skewers

HEALTH BENEFITS
Wild salmon is one of the healthiest foods for your child's brain, being a great source of the omega-3 fats known as DHA and EPA, which are essential for cognitive function and memory and may also boost mood. Salmon is also a great source of protein, helping to support growth and development and to stabilize blood sugar levels through the day – important if you want your child to stay focused and energized. The omega-3 oils are also anti-inflammatory, so can be useful for skin conditions such as eczema.

Mini squares of grilled salmon with cubes of fresh pineapple create a sensational little dish accompanied by a gorgeous sweet and tangy chutney. Keeping the fish bite-sized is a great way to encourage even babies to try something new, too. This dish can be served hot or cold.

250g/ 8oz skinless salmon
fillets, cut into 8 cubes
light olive oil, for greasing
¼ pineapple, cored and cut into
8 cubes
1 tbsp honey or agave nectar

CHUTNEY
1 tbsp olive oil

1 garlic clove, crushed
2cm/¾in root ginger, grated
1 shallot, finely chopped
4 tbsp apple cider vinegar
400g/14oz tinned chopped
tomatoes
a pinch of cinnamon
a pinch of ground cloves
2 tbsp raw cane sugar or xylitol

SERVES 4

PREPARATION + COOKING
30 + 40 minutes + marinating

STORAGE
Keep the fish in the fridge for
1 day and the chutney for 4 days.

SERVE THIS WITH...
coleslaw
mixed salad

1 To make the chutney, heat the oil in a pan and sauté the garlic and ginger for 1 minute. Add the other ingredients and bring to the boil. Simmer for 30 minutes until thick and sticky, stirring occasionally. Leave to cool.

2 Put the salmon in a dish and spoon over a little chutney, keeping the rest to serve. Put the salmon in the fridge for 30 minutes while soaking 8 mini wooden skewers in water.

3 Preheat the grill to high. Lightly grease a baking sheet with oil and line it with baking parchment.

4 Thread a piece of pineapple and salmon on to each skewer and put on the baking sheet. Drizzle the pineapple with honey, then grill for 5–6 minutes until the salmon is golden and cooked. Remove the skewers before serving.

030

creamy trout pittas

SERVES 4

PREPARATION + COOKING
15 + 1 minute

STORAGE
Keep in the fridge for 2–3 days.

SERVE THIS WITH...
sliced tomatoes
vegetable sticks
Almond Chocolate Butter on
  Apple Wedges (see page 73)

HEALTH BENEFITS
Trout is a nutritious oily fish, rich
in omega-3 fatty acids. Oily fish
is also a useful source of vitamin
D, which is commonly low in
children's diets and vital for
immune function, healthy bones
and teeth and preventing many
chronic diseases.

This creamy fish pâté is perfect as a sandwich filler, spread on little strips of toast or used to stuff mini pittas or baby potatoes. Smoked trout has a mild flavour, making it a popular choice for children and an ideal option if you're looking to increase their intake of oily fish.

200g/7oz hot-smoked trout
  fillets, skinned
4 tbsp crème fraîche
juice and finely grated zest of
  ½ lemon

1 small handful of dill, chopped
4 mini wholemeal pittas
1 tomato, finely chopped
freshly ground black pepper

1 Put the trout, crème fraîche, lemon juice and zest and dill in a food processor and pulse to form a chunky paste. Do not over-process. Season with a little black pepper.
2 Warm the pittas briefly in a toaster so they puff up slightly. Split the pittas along one side and spread a generous amount of the trout pâté inside each one. Scatter over a little chopped tomato and enclose to serve.

easy sushi rolls

These rolls contain avocado and vegetables.

1 large ripe avocado, pitted
1 tsp reduced-salt soy sauce
2 tsp lemon juice
a pinch of cumin
4 nori sheets
¼ cucumber, halved lengthways,
    deseeded and cut into strips
½ red pepper, thinly sliced
1 handful of alfalfa sprouts

DIPPING SAUCE
125g/4½ oz cashew nut butter
    or other nut butter
2 tbsp lemon juice
1 tbsp raw cane sugar or xylitol
2 tbsp reduced-salt soy sauce
1 garlic clove, crushed

1 Spoon the avocado flesh into a bowl. Add the soy sauce, lemon juice and cumin and stir together until smooth.
2 Put a nori sheet shiny side down on a sushi mat. Spread the avocado thinly over the sheet, leaving a 2cm/¾in strip at one end.
3 Put a line of cucumber, pepper and alfalfa across the upper half of the sheet. Using your fingers, dampen the edge of the sheet with water. Using the mat, roll up the sheet to form a sushi roll. Put the roll seam side down on a board. Repeat with the other sheets and remaining fillings. Using a sharp, serrated knife slice each roll into 6.
4 Put the dipping sauce ingredients in a blender and blend until smooth, adding up to 4 tablespoons of water to form a thick dipping consistency. Serve the rolls with the sauce.

SERVES 4

PREPARATION
20 minutes

STORAGE
Best eaten immediately. Keep the sauce in the fridge for 3 days.

SERVE THIS WITH…
strips of cucumber and pepper
tamari soy sauce, for dipping
Griddled Pineapple
  (see page 130)
natural yogurt

HEALTH BENEFITS
Sea vegetables are one of the richest sources of essential minerals, making them an excellent nutrient-dense food. Packed with iodine, which is important for the normal functioning of the thyroid gland and metabolism, they are also rich in folic acid, which is needed for the formation of healthy red blood cells, and magnesium, which acts as a natural relaxant and calming mineral.

032

crispy spiced prawns

These juicy prawns have a lovely crispy crust.

SERVES 4

PREPARATION + COOKING
15 + 7 minutes + marinating

STORAGE
Keep in the fridge for 1 day.

SERVE THIS WITH...
strips of naan bread
steamed vegetables
Coconut Jelly Squares
 (see page 127)

HEALTH BENEFITS
Prawns are a surprisingly good
source of omega-3 fatty acids,
which are important for a child's
brain development and also
valuable to maintain a healthy
immune system and healthy
skin. They contain high levels
of immune-supporting minerals,
especially zinc and selenium,
plus plenty of high-quality
protein – essential for the
production of white blood cells.

2 tbsp tikka paste
2 tbsp Greek yogurt
2 tsp lime juice
16 uncooked king prawns,
 peeled
light olive oil, for greasing
75g/2½oz/½ cup fine polenta

RAITA
225g/8oz Greek yogurt
1 handful of mint leaves
1 handful of coriander leaves
¼ cucumber, peeled and
 deseeded
freshly ground black pepper

1 Put the tikka paste, yogurt and lime juice in a container
and mix well. Add the prawns and coat in the marinade.
Cover and put in the fridge for 30 minutes. Meanwhile,
soak 8 wooden skewers in water for 30 minutes.
2 To make the raita, blend the yogurt and herbs in a
food processor. Grate the cucumber, squeeze the flesh
to remove as much liquid as possible, then add it to the
yogurt mixture. Season with black pepper. Cover and chill.
3 Preheat the grill to high. Grease a baking sheet with oil.
4 Put the polenta on a plate. Remove the prawns from the
marinade and toss in the polenta, shaking off the excess.
Thread 2 prawns onto each skewer and put on the baking
sheet. Grill for 6–7 minutes, turning occasionally, until
they are golden, crispy and cooked. Remove the prawns
from the skewers and serve with the raita.

ricotta, pear & walnut sandwiches

This is a wonderful sweet, nutritious sandwich option, combining protein-rich cheese, ripe pears and brain-boosting walnuts. The filling is great for wraps and pitta breads, too, and also makes a wonderful topping for wholegrain bagels for an afternoon snack.

2 ripe pears, cored and diced
a pinch of cinnamon
225g/8oz ricotta cheese

2 tbsp chopped walnuts
8 slices of wholegrain bread

1 Put the pears, cinnamon, cheese and walnuts in a bowl and toss gently.
2 Spread the mixture over half the slices of bread, top with the remaining slices and cut into halves or quarters to serve.

SERVES 4

PREPARATION
10 minutes

STORAGE
Keep in the fridge for 1 day.

SERVE THIS WITH...
vegetable sticks
fresh fruit
Courgette & Apple Cake
 (see page 84)

HEALTH BENEFITS
Walnuts are the best nuts because of their high omega-3 content, and they have long been regarded as a "brain food". Omega-3 essential fats are vital for the health and function of brain cells and have been shown to improve mood, learning and behaviour in children. Try to eat them raw to retain as much of the essential fats as possible.

tofu & cashew burgers

These protein-packed vegetarian burgers are perfect as an energizing lunch.

MAKES 12

PREPARATION + COOKING
15 + 25 minutes

STORAGE
Keep in the fridge for 3–4 days.

SERVE THIS WITH...
mixed salad leaves
wholemeal rolls
Tomato Chutney (see page 105)
fresh fruit
Almond Linzer Biscuits
 (see page 75)

HEALTH BENEFITS
Button mushrooms are a good source of antioxidants, copper, zinc and selenium, which are all important for a healthy immune system. They also contain important polysaccharides and beta-glucans – well known for supporting immune function. They are also a useful brain food – being rich in B vitamins, including vitamins B6, B12, riboflavin (B2), thiamin, niacin and pantothenic acid.

2 garlic cloves
1 small red onion
3 tbsp olive oil or melted
 coconut oil
100g/3½oz button mushrooms,
 finely chopped

1 small carrot, peeled and
 finely grated
1 tsp smoked paprika
75g/2½oz/scant ½ cup roasted,
 unsalted cashew nuts
250g/9oz firm tofu, drained

1 Put the garlic and onion in a food processor and blend until finely chopped. Heat 1 tablespoon of the oil in a frying pan and sauté the garlic and onion for 2–3 minutes until soft but not brown.

2 Add the mushrooms, carrot and paprika to the pan and cook for a further 2–3 minutes until soft. Pour the vegetables into a sieve to drain off any excess moisture.

3 Put the nuts in a grinder or food processor and process until finely ground. Put the tofu in the food processor and process until crumbly.

4 Put the vegetables, nuts and tofu in a bowl and season with black pepper. Shape the mixture into 12 little patties.

5 Heat the remaining oil in a frying pan and fry the patties in 2 batches for 3–4 minutes on both sides, or until they are golden brown.

babaganoush with pitta triangles

A tasty twist on the classic Middle Eastern dip.

1 tbsp light olive oil, plus extra
    for greasing
2 aubergines
2 garlic cloves
juice of ½ lemon
75g/2½oz goat's cheese,
    crumbled
60g/2¼oz tahini

1 tbsp parsley, chopped
freshly ground black pepper

PITTA CRISPS
2 wholemeal pitta breads
2 tbsp light olive oil
a pinch of paprika

1 Preheat the oven to 190°C/375°F/Gas 5. Grease a baking sheet with oil.
2 Prick the aubergines all over and put on the prepared baking sheet. Roast for 30–40 minutes until black and soft.
3 Peel off the skin and scoop the flesh into a food processor. Process with the remaining ingredients until smooth. Season with black pepper.
4 To make the pitta crisps, preheat the grill to high. Slice the pittas in half horizontally and cut into small triangles. Drizzle with the oil and season with paprika and pepper.
5 Spread the pitta triangles on a baking sheet and grill for 5–8 minutes until crisp. Remove from the grill and leave to cool. Spread the dip on the pitta triangles to serve.

SERVES 6

PREPARATION + COOKING
20 + 50 minutes

STORAGE
Keep the dip in the fridge for 2–3 days. Store the pitta crisps in an airtight container for 1 day.

SERVE THIS WITH...
vegetable sticks
Choc-Nut Lemon Bars
    (see page 81)
fresh fruit

HEALTH BENEFITS
Aubergines are packed with antioxidants, phenolic compounds, such as caffeic and chlorogenic acid, and flavonoids, such as nasunin. Nasunin has been shown to protect the fats in brain cells from damage, whilst chlorogenic acid has a range of health benefits, including being antimicrobial and anti-viral. A good source of fibre for healthy bowel movements, aubergines can help to ease constipation.

*quesadilla wedges

HEALTH BENEFITS
Spinach is the perfect energizing food for children, packed with iron, folate, B vitamins, vitamin K and magnesium, which are all important for building healthy blood cells. It is also a great source of the antioxidants vitamin C, E and beta-carotene, which are vital for supporting your child's immune health, plus calcium for building bones.

A fun alternative to a toasted sandwich, these tasty wedges are packed with protein as well as containing plenty of greens, which are a great vegetarian source of iron and B vitamins.

2 tbsp olive oil or melted
   coconut oil
150g/5½oz firm tofu, crumbled
a pinch of turmeric
a pinch of paprika
1 garlic clove, crushed
few drops of Tabasco
2 roasted red peppers in oil,
   drained and chopped

2 large handfuls of baby
   spinach leaves
1 tbsp chopped coriander
   leaves
60g/2¼oz Monterey Jack or
   mozzarella cheese, grated
4 flour tortillas
freshly ground black pepper

SERVES 4

PREPARATION + COOKING
15 + 25 minutes

STORAGE
Keep in the fridge for 1 day.

SERVE THIS WITH...
mixed salad

1 Heat 1 tablespoon of the oil in a frying pan and fry the tofu with the turmeric and paprika for 4–5 minutes. Add the garlic and Tabasco and cook for a further 1–2 minutes.

2 Stir in the peppers, spinach and remaining oil and sauté for about 1 minute until the spinach has wilted. Season with black pepper and stir in the coriander.

3 Put one of the tortillas in a frying pan over a low heat for 2 minutes. Spoon over half the tofu mixture and half the cheese. Put a second tortilla on top and press down hard.

4 Fry for 2–3 minutes on both sides until golden brown and crisp. Remove from the pan and repeat with the remaining tortillas. Leave to cool slightly before cutting into wedges to serve.

Ⓥ Ⓧ Ⓧ Ⓧ Ⓧ Ⓧ Ⓧ Ⓧ

cheese & sun-dried tomato polenta toasts

Crispy little polenta toasts flavoured with cheese and tomato make these perfect nutritious bites for small children.

SERVES 4

PREPARATION + COOKING
20 + 30 minutes + chilling

STORAGE
Keep in the fridge for 1 day.

SERVE THIS WITH…
coleslaw or mixed salad
low-sugar baked beans
Summer Berry Ice Cups
  (see page 125)

HEALTH BENEFITS
Polenta is a delicious gluten-free alternative to toast and a rich source of B vitamins, fibre and slow-releasing carbohydrate to help keep your child's energy levels sustained through the day.

1 tbsp light olive oil, plus extra
  for greasing
750ml/26fl oz/3 cups low-salt
  vegetable stock
125g/4½oz/scant 1 cup quick-
  cook polenta

30g/1oz Parmesan cheese,
  grated, plus extra for
  sprinkling
8 sun-dried tomatoes in oil,
  drained and chopped
olive oil or melted coconut oil

1 Grease a 20cm/8in square shallow cake tin with oil.

2 Put the stock in a pan and bring to the boil. Gradually add the polenta, stirring constantly. Reduce the heat and simmer, stirring, for about 10 minutes or until the polenta thickens. Add the oil, cheese and tomatoes and beat well.

3 Spread the mixture in the prepared cake tin and leave to cool. Cover with clear film and refrigerate for 2 hours until firm, then turn out the polenta and cut into 2cm/¾in pieces.

4 Heat the olive or coconut oil in a frying pan and fry the polenta pieces in batches for 2–3 minutes on each side until brown. Sprinkle over a little extra Parmesan to serve.

mediterranean potato cakes

Rich and full of flavour, these little potato cakes are delicious hot or cold.

250g/9oz floury potatoes,
    peeled and cut into chunks
60g/2¼oz/½ cup sliced pitted
    black olives
1 roasted red pepper in oil,
    drained and finely chopped
40g/1½oz Parmesan cheese,
    finely grated

1 tbsp finely chopped basil
60g/2¼oz/½ cup plain flour
2 eggs, beaten
125g/4½oz/heaped 1½ cups
    wholemeal breadcrumbs
light olive oil, for greasing
freshly ground black pepper

1 Put the potatoes in a large pan of boiling water. Simmer for 12–15 minutes until tender, then drain and pass through a potato ricer or mash. It should be quite dry.
2 Add the olives, pepper, Parmesan and basil to the potato and mix well. Season with black pepper.
3 Put the flour, eggs and breadcrumbs on separate plates. Shape the potato mixture into little "cakes". Coat in the flour, then the egg, then the breadcrumbs. Chill for 30 minutes.
4 Preheat the oven to 220°C/425°F/Gas 7. Lightly grease a baking sheet with oil. Put the potato cakes on the sheet and bake for 20 minutes until golden and crisp.

SERVES 4

PREPARATION + COOKING
15 + 35 minutes + chilling

STORAGE
Keep in the fridge for 2 days. Freeze uncooked cakes for up to 1 month, then cook from frozen.

SERVE THIS WITH...
steamed vegetables
high-quality meat or vegetarian sausages
Peaches with Berry Syrup (see page 128)

HEALTH BENEFITS
Parmesan cheese is an excellent source of protein and rich in bone-building phosphorous and calcium. It also provides plenty of vitamins B12 and B2, zinc and selenium. It is full of flavour but high in salt, so use in small amounts to enhance the taste and nutritional profile of a dish.

039

bean & cheese bites

Using tinned butterbeans makes these little bites an easy store-cupboard recipe. The Middle Eastern spice sumac adds a subtle citrus flavour.

SERVES 4

PREPARATION + COOKING
15 + 20 minutes + chilling

STORAGE
Keep in the fridge for 2 days.

SERVE THIS WITH...
Tomato Chutney (see page 105)
salad or steamed vegetables
Chunky Breadsticks (see page 87)
Apricot Oat Slices (see page 80)
fresh fruit

HEALTH BENEFITS
Butterbeans, like other beans and pulses, are packed with nutrients, fibre and protein – a combination that can help to stabilize blood sugar levels. Being a useful source of iron, they can help to avoid anaemia and fatigue. They are also a good source of the minerals manganese, zinc and magnesium, which are essential co-factors in a number of enzymes that are important in energy production.

400g/14oz tinned butterbeans, drained and rinsed
1 small courgette, finely grated
75g/2½oz Cheddar cheese, grated
1 tbsp tahini
3 eggs
light olive oil, for greasing
4 tbsp sesame seeds
200g/7oz/2½ cups wholemeal breadcrumbs
1 tbsp sumac

1 Put the butterbeans in a food processor and process until smooth. Add the courgette, cheese, tahini and one of the eggs, and pulse to combine. Scrape the bean mixture into a lidded container and chill for 30 minutes to firm up.
2 Preheat the oven to 220°C/425°F/Gas 7. Lightly grease a baking sheet with oil and line it with baking parchment.
3 Mix the sesame seeds, breadcrumbs and sumac together on a plate. Beat the remaining eggs in a bowl.
4 With damp hands, take 1 tablespoon of the mixture and roll into a walnut-sized ball. Roll in the breadcrumbs to coat, dip in the egg, then coat again in the breadcrumbs. Repeat to make 12 balls. Put on the prepared baking sheet and bake for 20 minutes until golden and crisp.

fig & goat's cheese bruschetta

This imaginative variation on cheese on toast mixes soft dried figs with creamy mild cheese.

8 dried ready-to-eat figs
2 tbsp balsamic vinegar
2 tsp raw cane sugar or xylitol
60g/2¼oz soft mild goat's
  cheese

8 slices of bread, such as rye,
  wholegrain or pumpernickel,
  about 1cm/½in thick
light olive oil, for brushing
freshly ground black pepper

1 Preheat the oven to 180°C/350°F/Gas 4.
2 Put the figs in a small pan with the vinegar, sugar and 4 tablespoons of water. Bring to the boil, then simmer for 5 minutes until the mixture is syrupy. Leave to cool, then cut the figs into small pieces with scissors.
3 Put the goat's cheese in a bowl, mash with a fork and then fold in the figs. Season with a little black pepper.
4 Put the bread slices on a baking sheet and brush with the olive oil. Put the bread in the oven for just 1 minute until it begins to crisp. Remove from the oven and spread with the goat's cheese mixture. Return to the oven and bake for 1–2 minutes until the cheese has warmed through and the edges of the bread are golden.
5 Leave to cool slightly before serving.

SERVES 4

PREPARATION + COOKING
15 + 8 minutes

STORAGE
Keep in the fridge for 2 days.

SERVE THIS WITH...
vegetable sticks
mixed salad
1 handful of berries or grapes
Lemon-Coconut Macaroons
  (see page 78)

HEALTH BENEFITS
Dried figs are good for the digestive system, being a good source of soluble fibre plus the enzyme ficin, which can be soothing for the digestive tract. A concentrated source of nutrients, including iron and calcium and natural sugars, they make a useful pick-me-up when energy levels are low.

041

stuffed tomatoes

Creamy hummus crammed into cherry tomatoes makes a fun finger food, perfect for little mouths. Using flaxseed oil in the hummus is an easy way to boost your child's intake of healthy essential omega-3 and 6 fats too.

SERVES 4

PREPARATION
15 minutes

STORAGE
Keep in the fridge for 1 day.

SERVE THIS WITH...
Squash Scones (see page 82)
mixed salald
Mango-Orange Crêpes
(see page 131)

HEALTH BENEFITS
Tahini (sesame seed paste) is a wonderful nutrient-rich food for growing children, especially any that lack a good appetite. Rich in zinc (a deficiency that has been linked to poor appetite), tahini is also a useful vegetarian source of protein, healthy omega fats and B vitamins to support energy levels.

400g/14oz tinned chickpeas,
   drained and rinsed
2 tbsp lemon juice
2 garlic cloves, crushed
½ tsp ground cumin

3 tbsp tahini
2 tbsp flaxseed oil
8 vine-ripened cherry
   tomatoes, cut in half
½ tsp smoked paprika

1 To make the hummus, put the chickpeas, lemon juice, garlic, cumin and tahini in a food processor and process until smooth and creamy. Blend in the oil. If the mixture is still too stiff, add a little water to form a thick purée.
2 Scoop out the centres of the tomatoes and discard. Spoon the hummus into the centre of each tomato. Dust with a little paprika to serve.

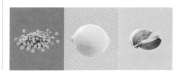

creamy dips

Dips are great eaten with crudites and breadsticks. Babies love them.

RED PEPPER ALMOND DIP
3 roasted red peppers in oil, drained
1 garlic clove, crushed
100g/3½oz/⅔ cup almonds
a pinch of smoked paprika
1 tbsp sun-dried tomato purée
3 tbsp flaxseed oil
2 tsp balsamic vinegar
1 tsp raw cane sugar or xylitol
salt
freshly ground black pepper

CARAMELIZED ONION DIP
4 tbsp light olive oil
2 red onions, thinly sliced
100g/3½oz crème fraîche
1 tbsp reduced-salt soy sauce
1 tbsp tahini
100g/3½oz Greek yogurt
freshly ground black pepper

SERVES 4

PREPARATION + COOKING
20 + 15 minutes

STORAGE
Keep in the fridge for 3 days.

SERVE THIS WITH...
a selection of vegetable sticks
Chunky Breadsticks
(see page 87)
Courgette-Apple Cake
(see page 84)

HEALTH BENEFITS
Rich in healthy monounsaturated fat, vitamin E and antioxidants, almonds are a protective, nutrient-dense food that are perfect for building healthy children. They are particularly high in calcium, which, together with magnesium, is important for nerve and muscle function and strengthening bones and teeth. An excellent protein source too, almonds can help to keep appetites satisfied and energy levels high.

1 To make the red pepper almond dip, put the peppers, garlic, almonds and paprika in a food processor and process to form a chunky paste. Add the remaining ingredients and process to form a smooth dip, adding salt and pepper to taste. Add a little more oil, if needed, to thin.
2 To make the caramelized onion dip, heat the oil in a frying pan and sauté the onions for 10–15 minutes until caramelized. Drain on kitchen paper. Mix together with the remaining ingredients and beat well.
3 Spoon the dips into separate bowls.

SNACKS

Mid-morning and mid-afternoon snacks are important for keeping children fuelled and will help to balance their blood sugar levels, enabling them to feel energized and alert. Instead of sugary sweets and drinks, opt for a snack that combines protein with some slow-releasing carbohydrate. Snacks are also a great opportunity to sneak some more fruit and vegetables into your child's diet, and here you will find a range of fabulous sweet and savoury ideas. Whether it's Chunky Breadsticks, Squash Scones or Pumpkin Seed Buns, or sweet treats like Cranberry Biscotti, No-Bake Whoopie Pies, Apricot Oat Slices or Lemon-Coconut Macaroons, you will be amazed at how healthy and delicious snacks can be.

peanut butter & coconut balls

MAKES 8

PREPARATION
10 minutes + chilling

STORAGE
Keep in the fridge for 3–4 days.

SERVE THIS WITH...
fresh fruit

HEALTH BENEFITS
Instead of ordinary honey or agave nectar, you could use manuka honey: a natural sweetener that may be beneficial when used occasionally and in small amounts. Being a natural antiseptic, it is useful for treating sore throats, coughs and colds. Also, being strongly anti-microbial, it can help to tackle bugs and viruses and has been used topically for wound healing. Honey should not be given to children under the age of one.

Little power nuggets, these sweet bites will help to re-energize your child when blood sugar levels are falling. Great for a mid-afternoon pick-me-up and an easy way to sneak in some additional omega-3 too.

2 tbsp crunchy peanut butter
1 tbsp flaxseed oil
1 tbsp honey or agave nectar
1 tbsp ground flaxseeds
60g/2¼oz/⅔ cup porridge oats

1–2 tbsp cocoa powder or raw cacao powder to taste
30g/1oz/⅓ cup desiccated coconut

1 Put the peanut butter, oil and honey in a bowl and mix to form a stiff paste. Add the flaxseeds, porridge oats and cocoa, and, using your hands, bring the mixture together to form a firm, slightly sticky paste.
2 Put the desiccated coconut on a plate. With slightly damp hands, roll the mixture into walnut-sized balls, then coat in the coconut. Put in the fridge to chill for 30 minutes to firm up slightly before eating.

almond-chocolate butter on apple wedges

A simple energizing snack that children will adore. Make up a batch of the almond chocolate butter and store it in the fridge. Healthier than any shop-bought versions, this is delicious as a spread on oatcakes and toast.

1 tbsp olive oil or melted coconut oil
1 tbsp raw cane sugar or xylitol
1 tbsp honey or agave nectar
175g/6oz almond or other nut butter

2 tbsp raw cacao powder or 1 tbsp cocoa powder
2 tsp pure vanilla extract
2 dessert apples, cored and cut into wedges

1 Put the oil, sugar and honey in a small pan and heat gently until all the sugar has melted. Add the almond nut butter, cacao powder and vanilla extract, then take the pan off the heat. Beat the mixture well until it is thoroughly combined and smooth.
2 Pour into a lidded container and leave to cool to room temperature.
3 Spread a little of the almond-chocolate butter on the apple wedges to serve.

SERVES 4–6

PREPARATION + COOKING
10 + 5 minutes

STORAGE
Keep the almond-chocolate butter in the fridge for 1 week.

SERVE THIS WITH...
glass of milk or milk alternative

HEALTH BENEFITS
Solid at room temperature, coconut oil is one of the best fats to cook with – that's because it is one of the only oils that can be heated to high temperatures without being converted into trans fats. It is also a great energy booster, as it is rich in medium chain triglycerides, which, rather than being stored by the body, are converted via the liver into immediate energy.

045

cranberry biscotti

These biscuits are sweetened with cranberries.

SERVES 4

PREPARATION + COOKING
20 + 45 minutes

STORAGE
Keep in an airtight container for
1 week.

SERVE THIS WITH...
fresh fruit

HEALTH BENEFITS
Cranberries are rich in the
antioxidants known as
proanthocyanidins, which appear
to help prevent urinary tract
infections by preventing bacteria
from attaching onto the urinary
tract lining. Similar effects have
been seen in other parts of the
body, too, making them useful
for preventing *Helicobacter
pylori* infection in the stomach
and dental decay. When buying
dried cranberries, choose those
without added sugars.

light olive oil, for greasing
40g/1½oz/scant ¼ cup raw cane
    sugar or xylitol
2 eggs
1 tsp vanilla extract
185g/6½oz/scant 1¼ cups
    almonds
a pinch of salt

2 tsp finely grated orange zest
½ tsp bicarbonate of soda
2 tbsp arrowroot or cornflour
60g/2¼oz/½ cup dried
    cranberries
30g/1oz/scant ¼ cup pistachio
    nuts

1 Preheat the oven to 180°/350°F/Gas 4. Lightly grease
a baking sheet with oil and line it with baking parchment.
2 Put the sugar, eggs and vanilla extract in a blender and
blend until smooth.
3 Put the almonds in a food processor and process to
form a very fine flour. Tip into a bowl with the salt, orange
zest, bicarbonate of soda and arrowroot. Stir in the egg
mixture, cranberries and nuts.
4 Shape the dough into 2 small log shapes and put on the
prepared baking sheet. Bake for about 30 minutes until
lightly golden.
5 Leave to cool for 15 minutes, then cut into 2cm/¾in
slices on the diagonal. Put the slices on the baking sheet
and return to the oven for 10–15 minutes until golden and
crisp. Leave to cool before serving.

almond linzer biscuits

These jam-filled biscuits are gluten free.

light olive oil, for greasing
250g/9oz/1⅔ cups almonds
225g/8oz/scant 1⅓ cups rice
    flour, plus extra for dusting
a pinch of salt
½ tsp xanthan gum

100g/3½oz butter
5 tbsp raw cane sugar or xylitol
2 tsp pure vanilla extract
75g/2½oz pure fruit strawberry
    or raspberry jam (no added
    sugar)

MAKES 12

PREPARATION + COOKING
15 + 10 minutes

STORAGE
Keep in an airtight container for
1 week.

SERVE THIS WITH...
fresh vegetable juice or fruit
  smoothie

HEALTH BENEFITS
Despite popular belief, butter is
actually a nourishing food for
children, since it is a useful source
of vitamin A and E to support
immune health as well as vitamin
D, which is vital for healthy bones.
Organic butter is a particularly good
source of conjugated linoleic acid
(CLA), which aids the body's use
of fat for energy. It also contains
butyric acid, a short-chain fatty
acid that has anti-fungal properties
and provides an energy source for
the cells lining the colon, reducing
inflammation and ensuring a
healthy digestive system.

1 Preheat the oven to 180°C/350°F/Gas 4. Lightly grease
a baking sheet with oil and line it with baking parchment.
2 Put the almonds in a blender and blend to form a fine
powder. Tip into a large bowl and add the rice flour, salt
and xanthan gum.
3 Melt the butter and sugar in a small pan over a low heat.
Stir into the flour with the vanilla extract and bring the
mixture together to form a dough. Roll out to 1cm/½in
thick between 2 sheets of baking parchment.
4 Using a 10cm/4in cookie cutter, cut out 12 rounds. Cut
out a small heart or circle from the centre of 6 of them.
5 Lightly press your finger into the centre of the complete
circles to make an indentation, then fill with a little jam.
Put the hollow circles on the top.
6 Put on the baking sheet. Bake for 10 minutes or until
golden. Cool for 10 minutes, then move to a wire rack.

chocolate cupcakes

These gluten-free cupcakes have a surprise berry jam centre.

HEALTH BENEFITS
Naturally sweet and bursting with vitamin C, strawberries are a popular fruit with children. They are also rich in soluble fibre, which is important for maintaining a healthy digestive system, and contain ellagic acid, which supports immune health. Finally, they are a good source of B vitamins, which are needed for a healthy nervous system, tackling stress and supporting energy levels.

60g/2¼oz/½ cup coconut flour
30g/1oz/¼ cup cocoa powder
½ tsp salt
1 tsp gluten-free baking powder
1 tsp bicarbonate of soda
5 eggs
125ml/4fl oz/½ olive oil or
    melted coconut oil

100g/3½oz/heaped ½ cup raw
    cane sugar or xylitol
2 tsp pure vanilla extract
100g/5½oz pure fruit strawberry
    jam (no added sugar)
200g/7oz dairy-free dark
    chocolate (70% cocoa solids)
6 strawberries

MAKES 12

PREPARATION + COOKING
20 + 30 minutes + freezing

STORAGE
Keep in an airtight container
for 3–4 days or freeze for up to
1 month.

SERVE THIS WITH...
fresh fruit

1 Preheat the oven to 180°C/350°F/Gas 4. Put 12 cupcake cases in a 12-hole cupcake tin.

2 Put the coconut flour, cocoa powder, salt, baking powder and bicarbonate of soda in a bowl and mix well.

3 Put the eggs, oil, sugar and vanilla extract in a food processor and process to mix. Gradually add the dry ingredients; continue to beat to form a smooth mixture.

4 Put a tablespoon of mixture into each cupcake case. Add 1 teaspoon of jam and cover with the rest of the mixture.

5 Bake for 20–25 minutes until golden brown and firm. Leave to cool in the tin for 10 minutes, then turn out and leave to cool on a wire rack.

6 Melt the chocolate in a heatprooof bowl set over a pan of simmering water, then drizzle over the cakes. Decorate with half a strawberry.

MAKES 14

PREPARATION + COOKING
20 + 15 minutes

STORAGE
Keep in an airtight container for
1 week.

SERVE THIS WITH...
fresh fruit

HEALTH BENEFITS
Xylitol is an ideal healthy
sweetener to use in recipes.
With 40% fewer calories than
table sugar and a low glycaemic
index, it has minimal impact on
blood glucose levels. This makes
it perfect for keeping energy
levels high through the day,
avoiding dips, which can affect
concentration. Xylitol has also
been shown to help maintain
healthy teeth.

lemon-coconut macaroons

These deliciously light, crisp, gluten-free
biscuits require minimal ingredients and effort.

light olive oil, for greasing
150g/5½oz/1¾ cups desiccated
    coconut, plus extra for
    sprinkling
5 tbsp raw cane sugar or xylitol

finely grated zest of 1 lemon
1 tbsp arrowroot or cornflour
3 egg whites
¼ tsp salt

1 Preheat the oven to 180°C/350°F/Gas 4. Lightly grease
a baking sheet with oil and line it with baking parchment.
2 Put the coconut and sugar in a food processor and
process to form fine crumbs. Put in a bowl and mix with
the lemon zest and arrowroot.
3 Put the egg whites and salt in a large mixing bowl and
whisk with an electric hand mixer until stiff peaks form.
Using a large metal spoon, fold the coconut mixture
lightly into the egg whites until thoroughly combined.
4 Spoon tablespoonfuls of the mixture onto the prepared
baking sheet, spreading out slightly to form 14 biscuits.
Bake for 10–15 minutes until lightly coloured.
5 Remove from the oven and leave to cool on the tray for
10 minutes before transferring to a rack to cool completely.

no-bake whoopie pies

Delicious biscuits that don't even need cooking!

light olive oil, for greasing
115g/4oz/scant 1¼ cups pecan
 nuts
115g/4oz/¾ cup cashew nuts
1 tbsp ground flaxseeds
3 tbsp melted coconut oil
a pinch of salt
finely grated zest of 1 lemon
2 tbsp raw cane sugar or xylitol

30g/1oz/¼ cup cocoa powder
115g/4oz/⅔ cup pitted dates

FROSTING
1 tbsp cashew or other nut butter
finely grated zest of 2 lemons
juice of 1 lemon
5 tbsp melted coconut oil
3 tbsp raw cane sugar or xylitol

MAKES 8

PREPARATION
20 minutes + chilling

STORAGE
Keep in the fridge for 1 week
or freeze for up to 1 month.

SERVE THIS WITH…
slices of fresh fruit

HEALTH BENEFITS
Pecan nuts are rich in
monounsaturated fats and
antioxidants, particularly
vitamin E, which helps to lower
inflammation in the body and
protect against chronic diseases.
They also contain a range of
minerals, including calcium
and magnesium, which have a
calming effect on the body as
well as supporting bone health.

1 Lightly grease two 8-hole whoopie pie tins with oil.

2 To make the biscuits, put the nuts in a food processor
and process to form fine crumbs. Pour into a bowl and
stir in the ground flaxseeds.

3 Process the remaining biscuit ingredients to create a
thick paste. Add the nuts and pulse to combine. Add 1
tablespoon of water to help bind the mixture.

4 Roll the mixture into 16 walnut-sized pieces and press
in the tin holes. Put in the freezer to harden for 30 minutes.

5 To make the frosting, put all the ingredients in a blender
and blend until smooth. Chill in the fridge for 15 minutes.

6 Remove the biscuits from the tin. Spread the flat side
of 8 biscuits with some of the frosting and then sandwich
with the other biscuits to form 8 whoopie pies.

Ⓥ 🅟 🅟 Ⓠ 🅞 🅞 🅟 🅞 🅞

apricot oat slices

Flapjack-style slices with an apricot filling.

MAKES 12

PREPARATION + COOKING
20 + 35 minutes

STORAGE
Keep in the fridge for 1 week
or freeze for up to 1 month.

SERVE THIS WITH…
natural yogurt
slices of fresh apricot

HEALTH BENEFITS
Orange juice is an excellent
hydrator and energizer,
rich in immune-supporting
bioflavonoids and vitamin C.
Oranges also contain the citrus
oil known as limonene, which
is known for its anti-cancer and
disease-fighting properties.

light olive oil, for greasing
250g/9oz/1¼ cups dried ready-to-
    eat apricots
125ml/4fl oz/½ cup orange juice
150g/5½oz/1 cup cashew nuts
225g/8oz/2¼ cups porridge oats

125g/4½oz/heaped ⅔ cups pitted
    dates, chopped
1 tbsp pure vanilla extract
150ml/5fl oz/scant ⅔ cup melted
    coconut oil

1 Preheat the oven to 190°C/375°F/Gas 5. Grease a 20cm/8in
square shallow baking tin and line with baking parchment.
2 Heat the apricots and orange juice in a small pan and
simmer gently for 5 minutes until the apricots are soft and
most of the liquid has been absorbed. Leave to cool slightly,
then blend using a stick blender to form a thick purée.
3 Put the cashew nuts in a food processor and process to
form a fine flour. Add the oats and pulse briefly to break them
down. Tip the mixture into a large bowl.
4 Put the dates, vanilla extract and melted coconut oil in a food
processor and blend to form a paste. Add to the dry ingredients
and mix well with your hands to form a crumbly dough.
5 Spoon half of the mixture into the prepared tin and press
down well with the back of a metal spoon. Spread the apricot
purée over it, then top with the remaining mixture. Bake for
25–30 minutes until golden. Leave to cool then cut into 12 bars.

choc-nut lemon bars

Packed with protein from the nuts and seeds and low in sugar, these gluten-free bars are full of energizing nutrients and slow-releasing carbs.

light olive oil, for greasing
juice and finely grated zest of
    3 lemons
115g/4oz/scant ⅔ cup pitted
    dates, plus 50g/1¾oz/heaped
    ¼ cup chopped pitted dates
4 tbsp raw cane sugar or xylitol
50g/1¾oz walnut or other nut butter
150g/5½oz/1 cup cashew nuts
115g/4oz/scant 1 cup walnuts
30g/1oz/¼ cup sunflower seeds

115g/4oz/heaped 1 cup
    gluten-free porridge oats or
    buckwheat flakes
50g/1¾oz/heaped ½ cup
    desiccated coconut

ICING
200g/7oz dairy-free dark
    chocolate (70% cocoa solids)
2 tbsp raw cane sugar or xylitol
2 tbsp walnut or other nut butter

MAKES 18

PREPARATION
20 minutes + chilling

STORAGE
Keep in the fridge for 1 week
or freeze for up to 1 month.

SERVE THIS WITH…
fresh fruit yogurt smoothie

HEALTH BENEFITS
Power-packed sunflower seeds
are rich in minerals such as zinc,
manganese, magnesium and iron,
as well as B vitamins to support
energy levels. They are also a good
source of vitamin E – an antioxidant
that keeps skin healthy and prevents
damage caused by toxins.

1 Grease and line a 30 x 20cm/12 x 8in shallow baking tin.
2 Put the lemon juice and zest, whole dates, sugar and walnut butter in a blender and blend to form a smooth purée.
3 Put the nuts in a food processor and process to form a flour. Tip into a large bowl, add the remaining ingredients and the date purée and mix thoroughly. Spoon into the prepared tin and press down firmly. Put in the fridge for 1 hour.
4 To make the icing, melt the chocolate, sugar and walnut butter in a pan. Pour over the base and spread thinly. Leave for a further 1 hour to harden. Cut into 18 bars.

squash scones

HEALTH BENEFITS
Butternut squash is rich in carotenoids, including lutein and zeaxanthin, which are essential nutrients for ensuring healthy eyesight. It is also a rich source of beta-carotene, the precursor for vitamin A, which supports the immune system and mucosal health, so useful for respiratory conditions. Squash is also rich in soluble fibre, which helps the digestive system to function smoothly. Finally, it is a good source of vitamin B6 and folate – important for the production of neurotransmitters in the brain and maintaining a healthy nervous system.

Moist and nourishing, these lovely little scones are filled with mashed butternut squash and mozzarella, making them an easy way to sneak a nutritious vegetable into your baby or toddler's meal. They are best served warm from the oven spread with a little butter or almond nut butter.

light olive oil, for greasing
250g/9oz butternut squash,
    deseeded and diced
300g/10½oz/2 cups wholemeal
    self-raising flour
1 tbsp baking powder
1 tsp raw cane sugar or xylitol

60g/2¼oz chilled butter, diced
50g/1¾oz mozzarella cheese,
    grated
1 egg, beaten
milk, to glaze
2 tbsp grated Parmesan cheese

MAKES 8

PREPARATION + COOKING
20 + 35 minutes

SERVE THIS WITH...
soup or Creamy Dips
    (see page 69)

1 Preheat the oven to 200°C/400°F/Gas 6. Lightly grease a baking sheet with oil.

2 Put the squash in a steamer and steam for 15 minutes or until tender. Transfer to a bowl and mash until smooth.

3 Put the flour, baking powder and sugar in a bowl. Rub in the butter with your fingertips until the mixture forms fine crumbs. Stir in the squash and mozzarella. Add the egg and knead to form a soft dough.

4 Turn out on to a lightly floured surface and knead gently. Press out the dough to a 2.5cm/1in thickness and stamp out 8 rounds with a 10cm/4in cookie cutter.

5 Put the scones on the prepared baking sheet and brush with a little milk. Sprinkle with the Parmesan.

6 Bake for 20 minutes until golden. Serve warm.

courgette & apple cake

This delicious moist cake, which is gluten free, combines chocolate with courgette and apple. For an extra treat, you could drizzle melted chocolate over the top.

SERVES 12

PREPARATION + COOKING
20 + 45 minutes

STORAGE
Keep in the fridge for 3–4 days or freeze for up to 1 month.

SERVE THIS WITH...
glass of milk or milk alternative

HEALTH BENEFITS
Courgettes have a high water content, which, together with their soluble fibre, makes them useful for treating constipation. They are also a good source of B vitamins, including folate, which is important for cell division and DNA synthesis. Courgettes, especially the golden varieties, are also rich in eye-supporting carotenes lutein and zeaxanthin.

4 eggs
115g/4oz/scant ⅔ cup raw cane sugar or xylitol
1 tsp pure vanilla extract
a pinch of salt
225g/8oz courgette, grated
2 apples, grated

200g/7oz/2 cups ground almonds
150g/5½oz/heaped ¾ cup rice flour
40g/1½oz/⅓ cup cocoa powder
1 tbsp gluten-free baking powder
115g/4oz/⅔ cup dairy-free plain chocolate chips

1 Preheat the oven to 180°C/350°F/Gas 4. Lightly grease a 20cm/8in cake tin or 900g/2lb loaf tin with oil and line it with baking parchment.

2 Put the eggs, sugar, vanilla extract and salt in a bowl and beat together. Stir in the courgette and apples.

3 In a separate bowl, mix together the remaining ingredients. Add the courgette mixture and stir to combine. Spoon the mixture into the prepared tin.

4 Bake for 35–45 minutes or until firm. Leave to cool in the tin for 5 minutes, then turn out onto a wire rack and leave to cool completely.

pumpkin seed buns

Little buns filled with pesto and grated cheese.

light olive oil, for greasing
150g/5½oz/1 cup self-raising
  wholemeal flour, plus extra
  for dusting
150g/5½oz/1¼ cups 00 flour or
  strong white bread flour
2 tsp raw cane sugar or xylitol
1 tsp baking powder
30g/1oz butter, chilled
150ml/5fl oz/scant ⅔ cup semi-
  skimmed milk

115g/4oz Cheddar cheese, grated
beaten egg, to glaze

PUMPKIN SEED PESTO
60g/2¼oz pumpkin seed butter
30g/1oz/¼ cup pumpkin seeds
30g/1oz basil leaves
1 garlic clove, crushed
1 tsp lemon juice
2 tbsp light olive oil
2 tbsp grated Parmesan cheese

1 Preheat the oven to 200°C/400°F/Gas 6. Lightly grease a 20cm/8in round shallow cake tin with oil.
2 Put the flours, sugar and baking powder in a bowl. Rub in the butter, then stir in the milk and mix to form a soft dough.
3 Knead the dough on a lightly floured work surface until smooth. Roll out to a large rectangle about 2cm/¾in thick.
4 Blend the pesto ingredients in a food processor to form a coarse paste. Spread over the dough. Sprinkle with Cheddar.
5 Starting from a long side, roll up the dough to form a Swiss roll. Cut into 12 slices and put in the tin in a single layer so they are touching each other. Brush with the beaten egg.
6 Bake for 30–35 minutes until golden brown. Serve warm.

MAKES 12

PREPARATION + COOKING
20 + 35 minutes

STORAGE
Keep in an airtight container for 2 days or freeze for up to 1 month.

SERVE THIS WITH...
homemade soup
vegetable sticks

HEALTH BENEFITS
Basil is a well-known anti-inflammatory herb that may be beneficial for conditions such as irritable bowel, inflammatory bowel and asthma. It is also anti-bacterial, so particularly useful if your child suffers with digestive upsets. Fresh herbs are more potent than dried and a great way to season dishes without the need for added salt.

teriyaki mixed seeds

SERVES 10–12

PREPARATION + COOKING
5 + 5 minutes

STORAGE
Keep in the fridge for 3–4 days.

SERVE THIS WITH...
fresh or dried fruit

HEALTH BENEFITS
Toasted seeds are a wonderful alternative snack to crisps and other processed savoury nibbles, like roasted peanuts, which are often high in saturated fats, trans fats and additives as well as added sugar and salt. Protein-rich seeds are a perfect choice to satisfy your child's appetite and keep them energized in between meals.

Seeds are a great source of essential omega-3 and 6 fatty acids and also contain plenty of protein, vitamins and minerals – all vital for growing children. A handful of seeds makes the perfect energizing snack. To make them more appealing to children, toast them with this simple Japanese-style sauce. Make a batch of them and store in an airtight container in the fridge.

100g/3½oz/heaped ¾ cup
  sunflower seeds
100g/3½oz/heaped ¾ cup
  pumpkin seeds

1 tbsp reduced-salt soy sauce
1 tbsp mirin
a pinch of raw cane sugar
  or xylitol

1 Put the seeds in a dry frying pan and toast gently for 2–3 minutes.
2 Pour over the soy sauce, mirin and sugar and stir to coat all the seeds in the marinade mixture. Keep stirring for a couple of minutes until the seeds are dry and golden brown.
3 Leave to cool before serving.

chunky breadsticks

Breadsticks are popular with children of all ages.

200g/7oz/1⅓ cups strong
    wholemeal flour
250g/9oz/2 cups 00 flour or strong
    white bread flour
15g/½oz dried active yeast
½ tsp clear honey
a pinch of salt

80ml/2½fl oz/⅓ cup light olive
    oil, plus extra for the garlic
    mixture, greasing and brushing
6 garlic cloves, crushed
1 tbsp balsamic vinegar
1 tsp raw cane sugar or xylitol
2 tbsp sesame seeds

1 Put the flours, yeast, honey and salt in a large bowl. Pour in the oil and 225ml/7¾fl oz/scant 1 cup warm water and mix with a wooden spoon to form a soft, springy dough.

2 Knead on a floured surface for 5 minutes. Put in an oiled bowl and cover with clear film. Leave to prove for 1 hour.

3 Preheat the oven to 200°C/400°F/Gas 6. Oil a baking sheet.

4 Heat 2 tablespoons of oil in a small pan and sauté the garlic for 2–3 minutes. Add the balsamic vinegar, sugar and 2 tablespoons of water and cook gently for 1 minute until soft.

5 Roll out the dough to form a large rectangle. Spread the garlic mixture over half of the dough and sprinkle with seeds. Fold the dough over and press down to seal.

6 Cut the dough into long strips, roll each to form a stick, then twist. Put on the baking sheet and brush with a little oil.

7 Bake for 20 minutes until golden brown. Leave to cool.

MAKES 8–10

PREPARATION + COOKING
20 + 25 minutes + proving

STORAGE
Keep in an airtight container for
4–5 days.

SERVE THIS WITH...
soup or Creamy Dips (see page 69)

HEALTH BENEFITS
Olive oil is rich in monounsaturated fatty acids and antioxidants, including phenols, which have been shown to help lower inflammation in the body, making it useful for treating conditions such as asthma and eczema.

DINNERS

Sharing a meal with your child is one of the best ways to encourage healthy eating as well as spending family time together. While all the recipes in this chapter can be eaten as finger foods, they can also be incorporated into main meals and are perfect for the whole family. There is a whole range of dishes to suit every taste, even for vegetarian or eaters. All the dishes are packed with healthy ingredients, protein, vitamins and minerals to support your child's growth and development. They have also been designed with our busy lifestyles in mind – simple and quick to prepare, so there is no need to spend ages in the kitchen.

chicken kiev patties

All the traditional garlic flavours, but smaller.

light olive oil, for greasing
250g/9oz skinless, boneless
  chicken breasts fillets,
  chopped
2 garlic cloves, crushed
4 tbsp herb- or garlic-and-herb-
  flavoured cream cheese
1 handful of parsley

50g/1¾oz/scant ½ cup plain
  flour
150g/5½oz/1½ cups dried
  breadcrumbs
20g/¾oz Parmesan cheese,
  grated
2 eggs, beaten
freshly ground black pepper

1 Preheat the oven to 200°C/400°F/Gas 6. Lightly grease
a baking sheet with oil and line it with baking parchment.
2 Put the chicken, garlic, cream cheese, parsley and
pepper in a food processor and process to form a chunky
paste. Shape into 8 patties.
3 Put the flour on a plate, the breadcrumbs and Parmesan
together on another plate and the eggs in a shallow bowl.
4 Coat the patties in the flour, then dip into the egg, then
coat with the Parmesan breadcrumbs. Place on the baking
sheet and bake for 20–25 minutes until crisp.

chicken wings with chilli tomato sauce

This is a healthy and delicious baked alternative to fast-food chicken pieces.

4 chicken wings
light olive oil, for greasing

CHILLI TOMATO SAUCE
2 tbsp Worcestershire sauce
2 tbsp raw cane sugar or xylitol

1 tbsp Dijon mustard
**1 red chilli, deseeded and
chopped**
1 garlic clove, crushed
500ml/17fl oz/2 cups passata

SERVES 4

PREPARATION + COOKING
15 + 45 minutes + marinating

STORAGE
Keep in the fridge for 2 days.

SERVE THIS WITH...
coleslaw
vegetable sticks
Banana Choc–Nut Bites
(see page 134)

1 Put all the ingredients for the chilli tomato sauce in a small pan. Bring to the boil, then simmer for 10 minutes to thicken slightly. Leave to cool to room temperature.
2 Trim the end off each chicken wing, then cut each in half through the joint. Put in a bowl and coat with a little of the sauce. Cover and marinate in the fridge for 1–2 hours. Put the remaining sauce in a bowl, cover and chill until needed.
3 Preheat the oven to 200°C/400°F/Gas 6. Put the chicken in a single layer on a greased rack inside a large shallow baking dish. Bake for 30 minutes or until the chicken is golden and cooked (the juices should run clear when the chicken is pierced in the thickest part with a skewer).
4 Serve the chicken wings with the remaining sauce.

HEALTH BENEFITS
Passata and tinned tomatoes are rich in carotenoids, including beta-carotene, which is necessary for the production of vitamin A. This is a vital nutrient for a healthy immune system and the maintenance of a healthy mucosal membrane – important for skin, respiratory and digestive health.

crispy chicken

This is a tasty "Southern fried"-style dish.

light olive oil, for greasing
8 small chicken drumsticks
50g/1¾oz/scant ½ cup plain
flour
3 eggs, beaten

200g/7oz/2 cups dried
breadcrumbs
1 tsp cayenne pepper
1 tsp dried thyme
1 tsp dried oregano
freshly ground black pepper

SERVES 4

PREPARATION + COOKING
20 + 30 minutes

STORAGE
Keep the chicken in the fridge
for 2 days and the sauce for
3–4 days.

SERVE THIS WITH
Chilli Tomato Sauce (see page 91)
roasted vegetables and potatoes
mixed salad
Griddled Pineapple (see page 130)

HEALTH BENEFITS
These crispy chicken bites are
baked with a minimum of fat,
making them a healthy option
for children. Most chicken finger
food at fast-food restaurants is
deep fried, which increases our
intake of not only saturated fats
but also trans fats, which have
been shown to be harmful to
our health.

1 Preheat the oven to 200°C/400°F/Gas 6. Lightly grease
a baking sheet with oil and line it with baking parchment.
2 Remove the skin from the drumsticks and score the
flesh lightly with a sharp knife.
3 Put the flour on a plate and season with black pepper.
Put the beaten eggs in a shallow dish. Mix together the
breadcrumbs, cayenne pepper and herbs on another plate.
4 Coat the chicken in the flour and shake off the excess.
Dip in the egg, then coat thoroughly in the breadcrumbs.
5 Put the chicken in a single layer on the prepared
baking sheet and cook for 25–30 minutes or until cooked
through (the juices should run clear when the chicken
is pierced in the thickest part with a skewer). Turn them
over halfway through cooking to ensure they are golden
all over.
6 Serve with a dipping sauce of your choice.

pomegranate-glazed chicken thighs

Sweet and sticky, these delicious chicken pieces are coated with a tangy Middle Eastern marinade made using pomegranate molasses.

4 skinless, boneless chicken
   thighs, cut in half
2 tbsp pomegranate molasses
2 garlic cloves, crushed

a pinch of cinnamon
light olive oil, for greasing
freshly ground black pepper

1 Put the chicken thighs in a shallow lidded container.

2 Mix together the pomegranate molasses, garlic and cinnamon in a bowl, and season with black pepper. Rub the mixture all over the chicken. Cover and put in the fridge to marinate for a few hours or overnight.

3 Preheat the grill to high. Lightly grease a baking sheet with oil.

4 Put the chicken thighs on the prepared baking sheet. Grill for 15 minutes until cooked through (the juices should run clear when the chicken is pierced in the thickest part with a skewer). Brush with any remaining marinade during cooking and turn to make sure the thighs are cooked and glazed all over.

SERVES 4

PREPARATION + COOKING
10 + 15 minutes + marinating

STORAGE
Keep in the fridge for 1 day.

SERVE THIS WITH...
steamed green beans and
   mangeout
corn on the cob
Apricot Oat Slices (see page 80)
fresh fruit

HEALTH BENEFITS
Garlic is a natural antibiotic and is antimicrobial, making it useful for protecting your child against infections including parasites and bacterial and yeast infections. It is also rich in sulphurous compounds that support liver detoxification and immune function. Being anti-inflammatory, it may also protect against asthma.

061

spicy chicken kebabs

A variation on a traditional Turkish shish kebab.

SERVES 4

PREPARATION + COOKING
15 + 15 minutes + marinating

STORAGE
Keep the kebabs in the fridge for
1 day and the sauce for 2–3 days.

SERVE THIS WITH...
4 wholemeal mini pitta breads
shredded lettuce
sliced tomatoes
Summer Berry Ice Cups
 (see page 125)

HEALTH BENEFITS
Flaxseed oil is rich in the
essential omega-3 fatty acids
and is a useful way of increasing
your child's intake, especially
for vegetarians. Omega-3
fats are crucial for cognitive
function because they form an
essential part of the membrane
of brain cells, important for
communication within and
between cells, aiding brain
function.

250g/9oz skinless, boneless
 chicken breasts fillets, cut
 into cubes
8 cherry tomatoes

MARINADE
3 garlic cloves, crushed
1 tbsp sun-dried tomato purée
4 tbsp natural yogurt
2 tbsp lemon juice
½ tsp salt
½ tsp raw cane sugar or xylitol

1 tsp smoked paprika
1 tsp grated lemon zest

SAUCE
150g/5½oz/scant ⅔ cup
 natural yogurt
4 tbsp tahini
½ tsp cumin
juice of ½ lemon
1 tbsp chopped mint
1 tsp flaxseed oil
1 garlic clove, crushed

1 Put the chicken in a shallow lidded container. Mix the
marinade ingredients together and pour over the chicken.
Cover and leave to marinate in the fridge for 1 hour or
overnight. Meanwhile, soak four wooden skewers in water
for 30 minutes.

2 Put all the sauce ingredients in a bowl and mix well.

3 Preheat the grill to high. Thread the chicken pieces and
tomatoes onto the skewers. Grill, turning occasionally, for
10–15 minutes until golden and cooked through.

4 Leave to cool slightly. Remove the skewers before
serving the chicken with the sauce.

thai-spiced turkey balls

Little balls of turkey packed with Thai flavours.

light olive oil, for greasing
200g/7oz turkey mince
1 lime leaf, shredded
1 lemongrass stalk,
    outer leaves discarded,
    finely chopped
2 tsp cornflour
4 spring onions, finely chopped
freshly ground black pepper

DUNKING BROTH
300ml/10½fl oz/scant 1¼ cups
    low-salt fresh chicken stock
2 shallots, finely chopped
1 red chilli, deseeded, chopped
2 tsp raw cane sugar or xylitol
1 tbsp Thai fish sauce
2cm/¾in piece root ginger,
    peeled and grated

SERVES 4

PREPARATION + COOKING
15 + 25 minutes

STORAGE
Keep the meatballs and broth
in the fridge for 2 days.

SERVE THIS WITH...
rice noodles
mangetout and baby corn
Mango Fruit Lollies
  (see page 124)

HEALTH BENEFITS
Turkey is a low-fat, protein-rich
food, often overlooked and
reserved for festive occasions
only. It is a good source of
zinc – an essential mineral
component of over 200 enzymes
in the body, essential for growth,
a healthy nervous system and
brain development. It is also rich
in B vitamins. All B vitamins are
crucial for mental health, and,
being water soluble, they pass
rapidly out of the body, so your
child needs a regular intake daily.

1 Preheat the oven to 200°C/400°F/Gas 6. Lightly grease
a baking sheet with oil and line it with baking parchment.
2 To make the meatballs, mix all the ingredients together
in a large bowl. Season with a little black pepper.
3 With damp hands, shape the mixture into 12 balls and
put on the baking sheet. Bake for 20–25 minutes, turning
twice during cooking to ensure they are golden brown.
4 Meanwhile, bring the broth ingredients to the boil in a pan
and simmer for 10 minutes. Dunk the balls in the broth.

asian-spiced duck

Strips of lean duck breast in a sweet, fragrant sauce are delicious and packed with protein.

SERVES 4

PREPARATION + COOKING
15 + 25 minutes + marinating

STORAGE
Keep in the fridge for 2 days.

SERVE THIS WITH
8 Chinese pancakes
strips of cucumber
shredded lettuce
hoisin sauce or tamari soy sauce
Sweet Cherry Samosas
  (see page 132)

HEALTH BENEFITS
Although honey is an intense
sweetener, it does possess some
health benefits, particularly if it
is unprocessed organic honey.
Rich in antioxidants, honey is
a natural antiseptic and useful
for coughs, colds and digestive
upsets. Use in small amounts
only and do not feed to babies
under one year old.

2 duck breasts, about 250g/9oz
  total weight

MARINADE
2 tbsp honey or agave nectar
1 tsp Chinese five spice powder
1 garlic clove, crushed
2 star anise
3 tbsp reduced-salt soy sauce
150ml/5fl oz/scant ⅔ cup
  low-salt fresh chicken stock
2 tbsp Chinese rice wine

1 Preheat the oven to 190°C/375°F/Gas 5.
2 Put the duck breasts in a bowl. Drizzle with the honey
and sprinkle with the five spice powder.
3 Put the remaining marinade ingredients in a small
pan and bring to the boil. Lower the heat and simmer for
5 minutes until syrupy. Leave to cool to room temperature.
4 Prick the duck breasts with a fork and pour over the
marinade. Leave in the fridge to marinate for at least
15 minutes.
5 Put the duck breasts on a wire rack over a large roasting
tin and roast in the preheated oven for 20 minutes, until
golden and cooked through.
6 Leave the duck to rest for 10 minutes, then shred into
thin strips to be used as a filling for Chinese pancakes.

crispy pork belly bites

A great finger-food alternative to a Sunday roast.

1kg/2lb 4oz boneless pork belly
1 tsp Chinese five spice powder
1 litre/35fl oz/4 cups low-salt
    fresh chicken stock

2 garlic cloves, crushed
250ml/9fl oz/1 cup apple juice
2 tbsp light olive oil
freshly ground black pepper

1 Preheat the oven to 180°C/350°F/Gas 4.

2 Rub the flesh side of the pork belly with the Chinese spice powder and season with a little black pepper.

3 Put the chicken stock, garlic and apple juice in a casserole dish that is large enough to fit the pork. Bring to the boil, then lower the heat to a simmer and add the pork. The pork should be submerged; if not, add a little water. Cover with a lid and cook in the oven for 3 hours.

4 Leave the pork to cool in the stock, then transfer the pork to a tray and leave to chill in the fridge for 1 hour.

5 Cut the pork into bite-sized squares. Heat the oil in a large frying pan. Add the pork, skin side down, and cook for 5 minutes until the skin is crisp. Turn over and cook for a further 2–3 minutes until the flesh is brown. Repeat until all the pork is cooked (probably 3 batches).

6 Drain on kitchen paper and serve hot or cold.

SERVES 8

PREPARATION + COOKING
15 minutes + 3 hours 30 minutes
+ cooling + chilling

STORAGE
Keep in the fridge for 2 days.

SERVE THIS WITH...
apple sauce
sweet potato wedges
steamed vegetable florets
Apple & Pecan Tarts
  (see page 139)

HEALTH BENEFITS
Pork is a great protein food, rich in a whole range of vitamins and minerals, including selenium, zinc, iron and magnesium, which are important for energy production and immune health. It also contains a wealth of B vitamins, which are vital for healthy brain function and tackling stress and anxiety.

pork satay sticks

Lean strips of pork coated in a creamy almond sauce create a delicious dish.

MAKES 8

PREPARATION + COOKING
15 + 25 minutes

STORAGE
Keep in the fridge for 1 day.

SERVE THIS WITH...
steamed rice
wilted greens
Griddled Pineapple
 (see page 130)
natural yogurt

HEALTH BENEFITS
Coconut cream provides plenty of lauric acid – the same fatty acid that is found in breast milk and is known for its anti-viral and anti-bacterial properties

175g/6oz almond nut butter or
 other nut butter
200ml/7fl oz/generous ¾ cup
 coconut cream
3 tbsp sweet chilli sauce
1 garlic clove, crushed

100ml/3½fl oz/scant ½ cup
 low-salt fresh chicken stock
1 tbsp lemon juice
450g/1lb lean pork fillet, cut
 into long strips
1 tbsp finely chopped coriander
freshly ground black pepper

1 Soak eight wooden skewers in cold water for at least 30 minutes. Meanwhile, preheat the oven to 180°C/350°F/ Gas 4.

2 Put the almond nut butter, coconut cream, sweet chilli sauce, garlic, stock and lemon juice in a small pan and bring to the boil. Reduce the heat and simmer, uncovered, for 1–2 minutes until the sauce thickens slightly. Leave to cool for 5 minutes.

3 Thread the pork strips onto the soaked skewers and put in a large shallow baking dish. Pour over half of the satay sauce. Bake for 20 minutes until cooked through.

4 Put the remaining satay sauce in a small bowl, season with black pepper and sprinkle with the chopped coriander. Remove the sticks before serving the pork with the sauce.

herby koftas

This is a quick and easy kofta recipe that can be prepared ahead and kept chilled until required. The pine nuts provide texture and additional minerals to the dish. This is a great energy booster, rich in protein, B vitamins and iron.

450g/1lb lean lamb mince
1 egg, beaten
½ tsp cumin
2 tbsp finely chopped mint
1 tbsp finely chopped parsley
4 tbsp pine nuts, finely chopped
1 garlic clove, crushed
1 red onion, grated
light olive oil, for greasing

1 Soak 12 skewers in cold water for at least 30 minutes.
2 Meanwhile, put all the ingredients in a bowl and mix together with your hands to combine. Form into 12 balls, and then mould around the end of each of the skewers to form little sausage shapes. Put on a tray and leave in the fridge to chill for 30 minutes.
3 Preheat the grill to high. Lightly grease a baking sheet with oil.
4 Transfer the skewers to the prepared baking sheet and grill for 10–15 minutes, turning frequently, until they are browned all over and cooked through.

SERVES 6

PREPARATION + COOKING
15 + 15 minutes + chilling

STORAGE
Keep in the fridge for 1 day.

SERVE THIS WITH...
Greek yogurt
wholemeal pitta breads
sliced lettuce and tomatoes

HEALTH BENEFITS
Pine nuts are incredibly rich in protein, making them useful for satisfying appetites and balancing blood sugar. They are also high in healthy monounsaturated fats, which can help to lower inflammation in the body. Packed with iron (a key component of haemoglobin, the oxygen-carrying pigment in blood that supplies energy), they are a great energizing food. They also supply plenty of magnesium, which helps to alleviate muscle cramps, tension and fatigue.

067

greek rissoles

Rissoles are little meat patties that make perfect finger food for children. Ideal for parties or for toddlers who are always on the go, these rissoles are packed with nutritious ingredients.

MAKES 12

PREPARATION + COOKING
15 + 25 minutes

STORAGE
Keep the rissoles in the fridge for 2 days and the sauce for 3–4 days.

SERVE THIS WITH...
mini pitta breads
vegetable sticks

HEALTH BENEFITS
Feta cheese contains less fat than many cheeses and has a lovely mild flavour that will appeal to children. It is a great way of adding more protein to dishes as well as providing bone-supporting calcium. Traditionally, feta was made with sheep's milk. If you can't obtain sheep's milk or goat's milk versions, choose one made from organic cow's milk to avoid antibiotic residues. It is high in salt, so use sparingly and do not add salt to the recipe.

light olive oil, for greasing
250g/9oz lamb mince
1 garlic clove, crushed
1 tbsp tomato purée
30g/1oz/¼ cup pitted black olives, chopped
60g/2¼oz feta cheese, crumbled
½ tsp cumin

30g/1oz/scant ½ cup wholemeal breadcrumbs
freshly ground black pepper

YOGURT SAUCE
150g/5½oz Greek yogurt
1 handful of mint leaves, finely chopped
1 garlic clove, crushed

1 Preheat the oven to 200°C/400°F/Gas 6. Lightly grease a baking sheet with oil and line it with baking parchment.

2 Put all the ingredients for the rissoles in a large bowl and mix together until thoroughly combined. With damp hands, shape the mixture into 12 little rissoles.

3 Put the rissoles on the prepared baking sheet and bake for 20–25 minutes until brown and cooked through.

4 Meanwhile, put the ingredients for the yogurt sauce in a bowl and stir well. Cover and leave to chill until needed.

5 Serve the rissoles hot, with a spoonful of the yogurt sauce drizzled over.

pesto & lamb frittatas

These tasty little bites include plenty of vegetables and chunks of leftover roast lamb.

light olive oil, for greasing
8 asparagus spears
30g/1oz/scant ¼ cup frozen
   peas
6 eggs, beaten
150ml/5fl oz/scant ⅔ cup
   double cream
1 courgette, grated

2 tbsp pesto
30g/1oz Parmesan cheese,
   grated
1 tbsp snipped chives
30g/1oz sliced roast lamb,
   diced
freshly ground black pepper

SERVES 4

PREPARATION + COOKING
15 + 30 minutes

STORAGE
Keep in the fridge for 2 days.

SERVE THIS WITH...
steamed vegetables or mixed salad
Squash Scones (see page 82)
Ice Cream Sandwiches
   (see page 126)
fresh fruit

1 Preheat the oven to 190°C/375°F/Gas 5. Lightly grease 8 holes in a muffin tin with oil.
2 Bring a saucepan of water to the boil. Add the asparagus and boil for 1–2 minutes to blanch it. Drain, then cut into bite-sized pieces.
3 Put the peas in a bowl. Pour boiling water over and leave to heat through for 2–3 minutes, then drain.
4 Put the eggs and cream in a bowl and whisk together, then stir in the remaining ingredients and season with a little black pepper.
5 Spoon the mixture into the holes in the prepared muffin tin. Bake for 20–25 minutes until golden and puffy on top. Leave to cool for 5–10 minutes before turning out.

HEALTH BENEFITS
Asparagus contains the amino acid asparagine, which is known to support detoxification and ease fluid retention, making it useful to help alleviate bloating as well as supporting liver and kidney function. It is also packed with folate – an essential B vitamin for the production of hormones and neurotransmitters in the brain. Asparagus is also rich in powerful antioxidants, including vitamin C, E and glutathione, to support immune health.

beetroot & beef mini burgers

Beetroot blends beautifully with lean beef mince to make wonderfully moist burgers that kids will love, making this another great way to sneak in extra vegetables.

MAKES 8

PREPARATION + COOKING
15 + 10 minutes + chilling

STORAGE
Keep in the fridge for 2 days.

SERVE THIS WITH...
wholemeal rolls or pitta breads
mixed salad leaves
Tomato Chutney (see page 105)
Peaches with Berry Syrup
  (see page 128)

HEALTH BENEFITS
Beetroot is well known as a blood-boosting food, being rich in iron and folic acid to help build up red blood cells and prevent fatigue and anaemia. It also contains nitrate, which the body uses to create nitric oxide, which is important for circulation and cardiovascular health. Folic acid can also help to lower levels of homocysteine – a toxic chemical that has been linked to a range of chronic conditions, including poor mental function.

450g/1lb lean beef steak mince
115g/4oz cooked beetroot in
  natural juices, drained and
  grated

1 shallot, finely chopped
light olive oil, for greasing
freshly ground black pepper

1 Put the mince, beetroot and shallot in a large bowl and season with black pepper. Mix together with your hands, then shape into 8 burgers. Put on a plate, cover and leave in the fridge to chill for 30 minutes to firm up.
2 Lightly grease a griddle pan with oil, then heat. Cook the mini burgers in batches for 3–4 minutes on each side, then serve.

meaty pasta slice

A delicious pasta bake cut into slices.

1 tbsp light olive oil, plus extra
    for greasing
225g/8oz lean beef mince
1 small red onion, finely
    chopped
1 carrot, peeled and grated
400g/14oz tinned chopped
    tomatoes

115g/4oz wholemeal macaroni
    or other small pasta shapes
6 eggs, beaten
115g/4oz Cheddar cheese,
    grated
60g/2¼oz Parmesan cheese,
    grated

1 Preheat the oven to 180°C/350°F/Gas 4. Lightly grease
a 23 x 30cm/9 x 12in shallow baking dish with oil.
2 Heat the oil in a large frying pan and fry the beef for
5 minutes, stirring occasionally. Add the onion and cook
for 2–3 minutes, then stir in the carrot and tomatoes and
bring to the boil. Simmer for 15 minutes, still stirring, and
adding a little water if too dry. Set aside.
3 Cook the pasta according to the instructions on the
packet, then drain. Add to the mince.
4 Put the eggs and Cheddar in a bowl and beat together,
then stir into the mince. Tip the mixture into the prepared
baking dish, sprinkle over the Parmesan and bake for
about 40 minutes until set and golden brown on top.
Cover with foil during cooking if it gets too brown.
5 Leave to cool in the dish, then serve in slices.

SERVES 8–10

PREPARATION + COOKING
20 minutes + 1 hour 20 minutes

STORAGE
Keep in the fridge for 2–3 days.

SERVE THIS WITH…
mixed salad
Frozen Pineapple Cheesecake
  Slice (see page 138)

HEALTH BENEFITS
The quality of the meat you buy
will greatly influence the nutrient
content of your dish. Meat that
has been reared organically or
free range will tend to be leaner
and richer in nutrients. Lean beef
mince is a protein-packed food
that supplies plenty of iron, zinc
and B12 – important for energy.
Zinc helps with cell growth,
improves immunity and speeds
wound healing. Vitamin B12
promotes the body's production
of red blood cells and helps
to keep the brain and nervous
system functioning at their peak.

071

beef & mushroom potato cups

Little potatoes make the perfect base for this creamy mushroom filling.

SERVES 4

PREPARATION + COOKING
20 + 30 minutes

STORAGE
Keep in the fridge for 2 days.

SERVE THIS WITH...
coleslaw
vegetable sticks
fresh fruit and natural yogurt
Peanut Butter & Coconut Balls
  (see page 72)

HEALTH BENEFITS
New potatoes are a low
glycaemic carbohydrate, which
means they release their sugars
slowly into the bloodstream, so
avoiding sudden highs and then
lows in energy levels.If you eat
the skin, you also increase the
fibre content. Potatoes are also
a good source of Vitamin C, B6
and potassium. B6 is vital for the
production of neurotransmitters,
including serotonin, which can
help to boost our mood.

12 small–medium potatoes
1 tbsp light olive oil, plus extra
  for greasing
6 button mushrooms, chopped
1 tsp wholegrain mustard
3 tbsp Greek yogurt
30g/1oz Gruyère cheese, grated
2 slices of lean roast beef,
  finely chopped
freshly ground black pepper

1 Put the whole potatoes in a steamer and cook until just tender, about 10 minutes. Drain and leave to cool.

2 Preheat the oven to 180°C/350°F/Gas 4. Lightly grease a baking sheet with oil.

3 Heat the oil in a pan and sauté the mushrooms for 2–3 minutes until soft.

4 Cut a thin slice from the top of each potato lengthways. Using a teaspoon, carefully scoop out most of the flesh from each potato. Put into a bowl with the mustard, yogurt, cheese, mushrooms and beef, and mash together. Season to taste with black pepper.

5 Spoon the filling into the potato shells and put on the prepared baking sheet. Put any excess filling in a small dish. Bake for 15 minutes until heated through. Serve warm.

coconut-salmon sticks with tomato chutney

A delicious healthy version of fish fingers.

450g/1lb skinless salmon fillets,
cut into bite-sized strips
30g/1oz/¼ cup cornflour
2 eggs, lightly beaten
115g/4oz/1¼ cups desiccated
coconut
50g/1¾oz/⅓ cup sesame seeds
light olive oil, for greasing
freshly ground black pepper

TOMATO CHUTNEY
250g/9oz vine-ripened
tomatoes, roughly chopped
5 tbsp cider vinegar
5 tbsp raw cane sugar or xylitol
50g/1¾oz/scant ½ cup raisins
1 red chilli, deseeded and
chopped
1 red onion, chopped

1 To make the chutney, heat the tomatoes, vinegar and sugar in a pan over a low heat, stirring until the sugar has dissolved. Add the remaining ingredients and simmer for 20 minutes until thickened. Leave to cool.
2 Preheat the oven to 200°C/400°F/Gas 6.
3 Pat the salmon dry. Put the cornflour on a plate and season with black pepper. Put the beaten eggs on another plate and the coconut and sesame seeds on a third.
4 Working in batches, toss the salmon strips in the cornflour, then egg, then coconut mixture. Transfer to a greased and lined baking sheet and bake for 20 minutes until golden. Serve hot or cold with the chutney.

SERVES 4–6

PREPARATION + COOKING
15 + 45 minutes + chilling

STORAGE
Keep the fish in the fridge for
2 days and the chutney for 1 week.

SERVE THIS WITH...
peas and corn on the cob
mixed salad
Banana Choc-Nut Bites
(see page 134)

HEALTH BENEFITS
Lycopene, a carotenoid and pigment that contributes to the red colour of tomatoes, is a major contributor to this fruit's health-promoting power. It is also an important antioxidant for protecting the skin from UV damage, reducing the risk of cancers, and protecting cells and tissue from free radical damage. As it is fat soluble, it needs a bit of fat to transport it into the bloodstream, so combining it with oily fish is perfect.

italian tuna balls

HEALTH BENEFITS
Tinned tuna is an excellent convenient protein-packed food for babies and older children. It also provides plenty of energy-boosting B vitamins, including B3 (niacin), which is important for balancing blood sugar levels, and selenium, for a healthy immune system. Tinned tuna is not, however, a good source of omega-3 fats, as the fats are destroyed during the tinning process.

A truly healthy alternative to fish nuggets and burgers, these nutritious little balls contain tinned tuna blended with ricotta cheese, basil and lemon zest to make a flavour-packed dish for children of all ages.

200g/7oz tinned tuna in olive oil, drained
115g/4oz/1½ cups wholemeal breadcrumbs
85g/3oz ricotta cheese
finely grated zest of 1 lemon
1 tbsp finely chopped basil
1 egg
freshly ground black pepper
plain flour, for dusting

2 tbsp olive oil or coconut oil

TARTARE SAUCE
6 gherkins, finely chopped
225g/8oz crème fraîche
2 tbsp chopped parsley
2 tbsp chopped dill
juice and finely grated zest of 1 lemon

SERVES 4

PREPARATION + COOKING
20 + 16 minutes + chilling

STORAGE
Keep in the fridge for 2 days.

SERVE THIS WITH...
vegetable sticks
Mediterranean Potato Cakes
  (see page 65)
Apple & Pecan Tart
  (see page 139)

1 Put the tuna, breadcrumbs, ricotta, lemon zest, basil and egg in a bowl and mix well. Season with a little black pepper.
2 Using floured hands, take small amounts of the mixture and roll into 12 walnut-sized balls. Dust lightly with flour.
3 Heat the olive oil in a frying pan and fry the balls in 2 batches over a medium heat for 6–8 minutes, turning occasionally, until crisp.
4 Meanwhile, make the tartare sauce by mixing all the ingredients together in a bowl. Serve with the fish balls.

074

polenta fish cakes

These crunchy fish cakes have a mild taste.

MAKES 8

PREPARATION + COOKING
15 + 30 minutes + chilling

STORAGE
Keep the fish cakes in the fridge for 2 days and the dressing for 3–4 days.

SERVE THIS WITH...
Tartare Sauce (see page 107)
steamed vegetables
Summer Berry Ice Cups
  (see page 125)

HEALTH BENEFITS
White fish is a high-protein food that is easily digestible for children. It is a good source of selenium and B vitamins, which can aid skin health and support a healthy immune system. White fish also provides iodine – essential for thyroid function and metabolism. Whilst white fish is lower in essential omega-3 fats than oily fish, it does contain some of these beneficial fats, particularly pollock and halibut.

200g/7oz floury potatoes,
  peeled and cut into chunks
115g/4oz cod or pollock fillet
115g/4oz smoked haddock fillet
1 shallot, finely chopped
150ml/5fl oz/scant ⅔ cup milk
1 tbsp chopped parsley
30g/1oz/scant ¼ cup rice flour
2 eggs, beaten
50g/2oz/⅓ cup fine polenta
light olive oil, for frying
freshly ground black pepper

1 Boil the potatoes for 15 minutes until tender.

2 Meanwhile, put the fish and shallot in a frying pan and cover with the milk. Cook for 3–4 minutes or until the fish is cooked through. Remove from the pan using a fish slice and leave to cool slightly on a plate. Discard the milk.

3 Remove the skin from the fish and flake the flesh into a bowl with the shallot.

4 Drain the potatoes, return them to the pan and cook for 1 minute to drive off the excess moisture. Mash well.

5 Mix the flaked fish and shallots into the potatoes. Stir in the parsley and season with black pepper.

6 With damp hands, shape the mixture into 8 small cakes. Coat each cake in the flour, dip in the beaten egg, then roll in the polenta. Cover and leave to chill for 30 minutes.

7 Fry the fish cakes in batches for about 3 minutes on each side until lightly brown. Drain on kitchen paper and serve.

creamy mackerel tarts

Your child will love these creamy little tarts.

1 recipe quantity Pastry
(see page 43)
flour, for dusting
1 tbsp light olive oil
1 leek, finely shredded
350g/12oz smoked mackerel,
skinned and chopped

3 eggs
200g/7oz crème fraîche
finely grated zest of 1 lemon
60g/2¼oz Cheddar cheese,
finely grated
1 tbsp dill, finely chopped

1 Preheat the oven to 180°C/350°F/Gas 4. Roll the pastry out on a floured surface and cut out 8 circles to line eight small tart tins.

2 Line the pastry cases with greaseproof paper and fill with baking beans. Bake for 10 minutes, then remove the beans and paper and cook for another 5 minutes to crisp the base. Remove from the oven.

3 Heat the oil in a frying pan, add the leek and fry for 3–4 minutes. Scatter the mackerel over the base of the tart tins, then add the leeks. Beat together the eggs, crème fraîche, lemon zest, Cheddar and dill. Pour the mixture into the pastry cases.

4 Bake for 20 minutes until set and lightly golden on top. Remove from the oven and leave to cool for 15 minutes before serving.

MAKES 8

PREPARATION + COOKING
20 + 40 minutes

STORAGE
Keep in the fridge for 2 days.

SERVE THIS WITH...
steamed broccoli
mixed salad
Griddled Pineapple
(see page 130)
natural yogurt

HEALTH BENEFITS
Mackerel is one of the best sources of omega-3 fatty acids to support your child's brain health and development. It is packed with nutrients, including vitamins B6 and B12, which are needed for red blood cell production, healthy nerve cells and the production of certain hormones and neurotransmitters. It is also one of the few good sources of vitamin D, which is essential for healthy bone formation.

076

SERVES 4

PREPARATION + COOKING
15 + 15 minutes

STORAGE
Keep in the fridge for 1 day.

SERVE THIS WITH
Tomato Chutney (see page 105)
vegetable sticks
corn on the cob
Chunky Breadsticks (see page 87)
Almond-Chocolate Butter on
  Apple Wedges (see page 73)

HEALTH BENEFITS
Shellfish are packed with
immune-boosting nutrients
to support your child's health,
including zinc, selenium and
plenty of protein. Zinc is also
important for growth and
development during childhood,
and activates areas of the brain
that are involved with taste and
smell. Low levels of zinc can be
linked to poor appetite. Zinc is
useful for treating childhood skin
conditions, including eczema.

prawn & tomato fritters

These crunchy, bite-sized fritters are made
from prawns and cherry tomatoes with a hint
of ginger. Delicious hot or cold.

225g/8oz raw peeled prawns
60g/2¼oz/½ cup plain flour
8 cherry tomatoes, chopped
1 tsp baking powder
2cm/¾in piece root ginger,
  peeled and finely grated

1 tbsp chopped coriander
1 egg, beaten
a pinch of cayenne pepper
2 tbsp olive oil or coconut oil,
  for frying
sweet chilli sauce, to serve

1 Put half the prawns in a food processor with the flour,
tomatoes, baking powder, ginger, coriander, egg and
cayenne pepper. Pulse until finely chopped.
2 Roughly chop the remaining prawns and add to the
mixture.
3 Heat half the olive oil in a frying pan. Drop 4 separate
tablespoonfuls of the mixture into the oil and fry on each
side for 2–3 minutes until golden brown. Drain on kitchen
paper. Repeat with the remaining oil and mixture to make
8 fritters.
4 Serve with the sweet chilli sauce.

risotto cheese balls

These rice balls contain spinach and cheese.

3 tbsp light olive oil
1 small onion, finely chopped
2 garlic cloves, crushed
115g/4oz/½ cup risotto rice
500ml/17fl oz/2 cups hot low-
    salt fresh vegetable stock
6 sun-dried tomatoes in oil,
    drained and chopped

115g/4oz baby leaf spinach
2 tbsp grated Parmesan cheese
200g/7oz mozzarella ball, cut
    into 8 pieces
1 egg, beaten
115g/4oz/¾ cup fine polenta

1 Heat 1 tablespoon of the oil in a large frying pan and cook the onion over a low heat for 5 minutes. Add the garlic and cook for 1 minute.

2 Stir in the rice, then gradually pour in the stock, one ladleful at a time, stirring constantly until absorbed.

3 Add the tomatoes, spinach and Parmesan and stir well. Season with black pepper and leave to cool for 1 hour.

4 Shape the mixture into 8 balls and push a piece of mozzarella into the centre of each one. Flatten the balls slightly to form small cakes. Leave to chill for 30 minutes.

5 Put the beaten egg on one plate and the polenta on another. Dip the balls in the egg, then in the polenta.

6 Heat the remaining olive oil in a frying pan and cook the cakes in 2 batches for 4–5 minutes on each side or until golden. Drain on kitchen paper and serve.

SERVES 4

PREPARATION + COOKING
20 + 40 minutes + cooling + chilling

STORAGE
Keep in the fridge for 1 day.

SERVE THIS WITH...
Chilli Tomato Sauce (see page 91)
steamed vegetables
Frozen Blueberry & Chocolate Slice (see page 135)

HEALTH BENEFITS
Mozzarella cheese is relatively low fat and a rich source of protein and calcium. Just 30g/1oz contains around 180mg calcium – over one-third of a young child's recommended daily intake. It also provides plenty of tryptophan, an amino acid that the body converts into serotonin, an important neurotransmitter for boosting mood.

vegetable samosas

Oven-baked samosas make a healthy meal.

SERVES 4

PREPARATION + COOKING
20 + 30 minutes

STORAGE
Keep in the fridge for 2 days.

SERVE THIS WITH
Raita (see page 58)
steamed green vegetables
Mango Fruit Lollies (see page 124)
Lemon-Coconut Macaroons (see page 78)

HEALTH BENEFITS
A highly nutritious alternative to ordinary potatoes, sweet potatoes are packed with antioxidants vitamin C and beta-carotene. Beta-carotene is converted by the body to vitamin A, which has anti-viral and skin-protecting properties. Sweet potatoes are also a rich source of vitamin E, and, being high in soluble fibre, can help to support digestive health.

1 tbsp light olive oil, plus extra for greasing and brushing
1 small red onion, chopped
1 garlic clove, crushed
1 tbsp medium curry paste
1 carrot, peeled and finely diced
1 small sweet potato, peeled and finely diced
100ml/3½fl oz/scant ½ cup low-salt fresh vegetable stock
30g/1oz/scant ¼ cup frozen peas
4 filo pastry sheets, cut into 3

1 Heat the oil in a frying pan and sauté the onion for 2–3 minutes until soft. Stir in the garlic and curry paste, then add the carrot, sweet potato and vegetable stock. Bring to the boil, then simmer until tender and all the moisture has evaporated. Stir in the peas, then leave to cool.
3 Preheat the oven to 200°C/400°F/Gas 6. Lightly grease two baking sheets with oil.
4 Brush each strip of filo with oil. Put a spoonful of mixture on each strip and fold over into a triangle. Keep folding over until each strip is used up. Brush with oil.
5 Bake 6 triangles per sheet for 20 minutes until crisp.

sweet potato falafels

These energizing bites are gluten free.

light olive oil, for greasing
1 sweet potato
150g/5½oz firm tofu, drained
1 roasted red pepper in oil,
   drained and chopped
1 tsp cumin
1 garlic clove, crushed
1 tsp ground coriander
1 tbsp chopped coriander
1 tbsp lemon juice

60g/2¼oz/½ cup gram flour
115g/4oz/¾ cup sesame seeds
freshly ground black pepper

TAHINI YOGURT DRESSING
1 tbsp tahini
2 tbsp natural yogurt
1 tbsp lemon juice
1 tsp raw cane sugar or xylitol

1 Preheat the oven to 220°C/425°F/Gas 7. Lightly grease
a baking sheet with oil and line it with baking parchment.
2 Roast the sweet potato in the oven for 45 minutes until
tender. Leave until cool enough to handle, then peel.
3 Put all the ingredients, except the sesame seeds, in a
large bowl and mash with a potato masher. Season with
black pepper. If the mixture is wet, add a little more flour.
Leave in the fridge for 30 minutes to firm up.
4 Heat the oven to 200°C/400°F/Gas 6. Put the seeds on a
plate. Mould the mixture into 12 balls, then roll in the seeds
and put on the sheet. Bake for 15 minutes until crisp.
5 Mix the dressing ingredients together and leave to chill
until needed. Serve the falafels hot or cold with the dressing.

SERVES 4

PREPARATION + COOKING
20 minutes + 1 hour + chilling

STORAGE
Keep in the fridge for 2 days.

SERVE THIS WITH...
warm wholemeal pitta breads
mixed salad
Fruit Slice (see page 136)

HEALTH BENEFITS
Gram flour, is simply dried
chickpeas ground to a flour-like
consistency. It is wheat and
gluten free and easy to digest.
High in fibre and protein, it is
perfect for balancing blood
sugar. It is also a rich source
of vitamin A, vitamin K for bone
health and several B vitamins,
including thiamin, riboflavin,
niacin, pantothenic acid and
folate. A good vegetarian source
of iron, too, with 115g/4oz/1 cup
supplying 4.5mg: over half the
daily requirement for children.

*crispy tofu skewers

HEALTH BENEFITS
Tofu is an excellent source of protein, providing all the essential amino acids for growth and development. It is also a useful source of omega-3 fatty acids for vegetarians and contains plenty of B vitamins, calcium and iron.

These chunks of tofu are coated in a sweet tomato soy marinade and covered with sesame seeds to create a crispy crumb. This is an energizing protein-packed meal with nutrients to support your child's growth.

2 tbsp tamari soy sauce
1 tbsp honey or agave nectar
1 tbsp light olive oil, plus extra
   for greasing
1 tbsp tomato purée
½ tsp wholegrain mustard

a pinch of cayenne pepper
450g/1lb firm tofu, drained
   and cut into 2cm/¾in cubes
60g/2¼oz/heaped ⅓ cup
   sesame seeds

SERVES 4

PREPARATION + COOKING
15 + 10 minutes + marinating

STORAGE
Keep in the fridge for 2 days.

SERVE THIS WITH...
Tomato Chutney (see page 105)
mixed salad leaves
cucumber sticks
baby corn

1 To make the marinade, mix together the soy sauce, honey, oil, tomato purée, mustard and cayenne pepper. Put the tofu in a shallow dish and pour over the marinade. Stir to coat thoroughly. Leave to marinate in the fridge for at least 1 hour or overnight.

2 Meanwhile, soak eight wooden skewers in water for 30 minutes.

3 Preheat the grill to high. Lightly grease a baking sheet with oil and line it with baking parchment.

4 Put the sesame seeds on a plate. Thread the tofu on the soaked skewers, then roll in the sesame seeds to coat.

5 Put the skewers on the prepared baking sheet and grill for 5 minutes on each side until golden and crispy. Remove the skewers before serving.

butterbean burgers

These creamy burgers contain a touch of pesto, which gives them a lovely summery Mediterranean flavour. Butterbeans are soft textured and mild in flavour, making them an ideal vegetarian protein food for babies and young children. Easy to make, these burgers can also be baked in the oven from frozen. Serve in little buns for a healthy fun meal.

SERVES 4

PREPARATION + COOKING
15 + 40 minutes

STORAGE
Keep in the fridge for 2 days or freeze for up to 1 month.

SERVE THIS WITH...
small wholemeal buns
mixed salad
sliced tomato
Frozen Pineapple Cheesecake slice (see page 138)

HEALTH BENEFITS
Red onions are particularly high in quercetin – a powerful antioxidant that can help reduce inflammation and lower histamine, making it beneficial for tackling allergies. Red onion is also a good source of chromium – a mineral needed to metabolize carbohydrates and balance blood sugar levels.

light olive oil, for greasing
820g/1lb 13oz tinned
    butterbeans, drained
    and rinsed
3 tbsp red pesto
1 egg, beaten
150g/5oz/scant 2 cups
    wholemeal breadcrumbs
1 red onion, grated
freshly ground black pepper

1 Preheat the oven to 220°C/425°F/Gas 7. Lightly grease a baking sheet with oil and line it with baking parchment.
2 Put the beans and pesto in a food processor and pulse until smooth. Add the egg, breadcrumbs and onion and pulse to mix. Season with black pepper.
3 With damp hands, shape the mixture into 8 little burgers. Put on the prepared baking sheet and bake for 30–40 minutes until golden and crisp. Serve hot.

almond pizza

This is a delicious alternative to regular pizza.

250ml/9fl oz/1 cup passata
6 cherry tomatoes, halved
½ red onion, thinly sliced
3 roasted red peppers in oil,
   drained and chopped
30g/1oz/¼ cup pitted sliced
   black olives
200g/7oz ball buffalo mozzarella
   cheese, torn into pieces
60g/2¼oz Cheddar cheese,
   grated

BASE
150g/5½oz/heaped 1¾ cups
   wholemeal breadcrumbs
2 garlic cloves, crushed
100g/3½oz/1 cup ground
   almonds
100g/3½oz/heaped 1 cup flaked
   almonds
115g/4oz unsalted butter,
   melted
2 eggs, beaten

SERVES 8

PREPARATION + COOKING
20 + 25 minutes

STORAGE
Keep in the fridge for 2 days.

SERVE THIS WITH...
mixed salad
vegetable sticks
Peaches with Berry Syrup
  (see page 128)

HEALTH BENEFITS
The Mediterranean vegetables –
peppers, tomatoes, red onion,
olives and garlic – used in
this dish are well known for
their anti-inflammatory and
antioxidant properties, which
can help with common conditions
such as asthma and skin
complaints, including eczema.

1 Preheat the oven to 180°C/350°F/Gas 4. Lightly grease a
32 x 23cm/13 x 9in Swiss roll tin with oil and line it with
baking parchment.

2 To make the base, put all the ingredients in a large bowl
and mix well, then press onto the prepared tin to form a
thin crust.

3 Bake for 10 minutes until just lightly coloured.

4 Spread the passata over the base, then top with the
remaining ingredients.

5 Bake for 10–15 minutes until the cheese is bubbling.
Leave to cool slightly, then cut into slices to serve.

tapas soufflé omelette

This chunky, fluffy omelette can be cut into wedges, making it ideal finger food.

SERVES 4

PREPARATION + COOKING
10 + 5 minutes

STORAGE
Keep in the fridge for 1 day.

SERVE THIS WITH...
mixed salad
Squash Scones (see page 82)
fresh fruit
natural yogurt

HEALTH BENEFITS
Globe artichokes have detoxifying qualities and help the liver function more efficiently. This is particularly useful if your child suffers with any allergies, poor skin or inflammation. Compounds in the artichoke increase the production of bile, which aids digestion, so may help to alleviate irritable bowel or tummy troubles.

6 eggs, separated
30g/1oz feta cheese, crumbled
4 marinated artichoke hearts in oil, drained and chopped
1 roasted red pepper in oil, drained and chopped
30g/1oz marinated mushrooms, sliced
1 tbsp chopped chives
1 tbsp olive oil or coconut oil, for frying
freshly ground black pepper

1 Put the egg yolks in a bowl and beat well. Stir in the feta and vegetables. Season with a little black pepper.
2 Put the egg whites in a separate bowl and whisk with an electric hand mixer until stiff peaks form. Fold the egg yolk mixture into the egg whites, being careful not to knock out the air. Sprinkle in the chives.
3 Preheat the grill to high. Heat the oil in a frying pan. Pour in the egg mixture and cook for 1–2 minutes. Put the pan under the hot grill and cook for 2 minutes until golden brown. Remove from the pan and cut into wedges to serve.

mini vegetable quiches

These quiches are delicious hot or cold.

1 recipe quantity Pastry
   (see page 43)
300g/10½oz purple or green
   sprouting broccoli, cut into
   2cm/¾in pieces
1 garlic clove, crushed
1 tbsp light olive oil
250g/9oz crème fraîche
4 eggs
8 sunblush tomatoes in oil,
   drained and finely chopped
freshly ground black pepper

MAKES 4

PREPARATION + COOKING
20 + 45 minutes + chilling
+ freezing

STORAGE
Keep in the fridge for 2 days
or freeze for up to 1 month.

SERVE THIS WITH...
mixed salad
vegetable sticks
Ice Cream Sandwiches
   (see page 126)

HEALTH BENEFITS
When you use 100% wholemeal
products, the wheat bran and
germ remain. These are packed
with health-promoting nutrients,
including selenium, magnesium,
B vitamins and manganese. You
also increase the fibre intake
and slow down the rate at which
sugars are broken down and
released into the bloodstream.
This helps to keep you feeling
fuller for longer and helps to
prevent mid-morning and mid-
afternoon energy slumps.

1 Roll the pastry out on a floured surface and cut out 4
circles to line four tartlet tins 8cm/3in in diameter. Put the
pastry cases in the freezer for 15 minutes. Meanwhile,
preheat the oven to 190°C/375°F/Gas 5.

2 Line the cases with baking parchment and fill with
baking beans. Bake for 10 minutes. Remove the beans
and paper and bake for a further 5 minutes. Remove from
the oven. Reduce the temperature to 180°C/350°F/Gas 4.

3 To make the filling, blanch the broccoli in boiling water
for 1 minute, then drain and dry with a tea towel.

4 Sauté the garlic in the oil for 1 minute, then add the
broccoli and stir for 1 minute. Season with black pepper.

5 Beat together the crème fraîche and eggs until smooth,
then add the broccoli and garlic. Stir in the tomatoes.

6 Spoon the filling into the pastry cases and bake for
20–25 minutes or until set and golden on top.

MAKES 8

PREPARATION + COOKING
20 + 20 minutes

STORAGE
Keep in the fridge for 2 days.

SERVE THIS WITH...
sweet potato wedges baked in
 olive oil
baby sweetcorn
mangetout
Coconut Jelly Squares
 (see page 127)

HEALTH BENEFITS
Red peppers contain high levels
of the antioxidants vitamin C,
beta-carotene, vitamin E and
zinc to help support immune
health. Vitamin C and the
magnesium in peppers are
important for tackling stress and
boosting energy production. The
carotenoids present, such as
lutein and zeaxanthin, are also
vital for healthy eyesight.

mixed pepper tartlets

These make wonderful party and picnic food.

1 tbsp light olive oil, plus extra
 for greasing and brushing
8 filo pastry sheets
1 red pepper, halved and
 deseeded
1 yellow pepper, halved and
 deseeded

1 tomato, diced
1 tsp balsamic vinegar
175g/6oz ricotta cheese
2 tbsp chopped basil
1 garlic clove, crushed
freshly ground black pepper

1 Preheat the oven to 180°C/350°F/Gas 4. Lightly grease
8 holes in a muffin tin with oil.
2 Cut a sheet of filo pastry into 4 squares and brush
with a little oil. Stack the 4 squares on top of each other
at different angles. Push the stack into a muffin hole and
brush again with oil. Repeat with the remaining filo sheets.
3 Bake for 8–10 minutes until golden. Leave to cool in
the tin for 5 minutes, then transfer to a wire rack to cool.
4 Grill the pepper halves, cut side down, on a baking
sheet for about 8 minutes until blackened. Leave to cool
for 5 minutes, then peel away the skin and dice the flesh.
Put in a bowl with the tomato, oil and vinegar and season
with black pepper.
5 Blend the ricotta, basil and garlic in a food processor.
Put a spoonful in each tart, top with the pepper mixture.

carrot & cheese roulade

This is a light but protein-rich dish.

**1 tbsp olive oil, plus extra for
   greasing**
200g/7oz carrot, grated
200g/7oz courgette, grated
4 eggs, separated

1 tbsp chopped parsley
**30g/1oz Parmesan cheese,
   finely grated**
250g/9oz herby cream cheese
freshly ground black pepper

1 Preheat the oven to 200°C/400°F/Gas 6. Lightly grease
and line a 30 x 20cm/12 x 10in Swiss roll tin.

2 Sauté the carrot and courgette in oil for 2–3 minutes
until soft. Spoon into a colander to drain and leave to cool.

3 Transfer to a bowl and beat in the egg yolks and parsley.
Season to taste with black pepper.

4 Put the egg whites in a separate bowl and whisk with an
electric hand mixer until stiff peaks form. Stir a spoonful
into the carrot mixture to loosen it, then fold in the rest.

5 Gently spoon the mixture into the prepared tin. Bake for
12–15 minutes until light golden brown and firm.

6 Put a large sheet of non-stick baking parchment on the
work surface and sprinkle with the Parmesan cheese.
Carefully turn the roulade out onto the sheet and cover
the top with a clean tea towel. Leave the roulade to cool.

7 Gently spread the roulade with the soft cheese, leaving a
1cm/⅜in border. Roll up from a short side. Slice to serve.

SERVES 8

PREPARATION + COOKING
15 + 20 minutes

STORAGE
Keep in the fridge for 2 days.

SERVE THIS WITH…
vegetable sticks
Chunky Breadsticks (see page 87)
Mango-Orange Crêpes
  (see page 131)

HEALTH BENEFITS
Beta-carotene-rich foods such
as carrots are excellent for
children's immune and skin
health. Beta-carotene is a
precursor to vitamin A, which
is strongly anti-viral. They are
important for the production
of T cells in the digestive tract,
which help the immune system
to respond appropriately to
beneficial bacteria and harmful
microbes and protect mucosal
surfaces against infection.

DESSERTS

The recipes in this chapter show you how easy it is to create delicious puddings and desserts that are healthy and nourishing. All the dishes included are based on fruit, whole grains, nuts and seeds, and are either naturally sugar free or use just a small amount of sugar. They include plenty of protein to help keep blood sugar levels balanced, avoiding the sugar highs and lows often associated with children's sweet treats. There are many delicious options to choose from, such as cooling Mango Fruit Lollies and Ice Cream Sandwiches, as well as Sweet Cherry Samosas and Banana Choc-Nut Bites. The whole family will adore these scrumptious dishes – desserts will never be the same again!

mango fruit lollies

Tropical ripe mangoes are naturally sweet and bursting with nutrients to keep your baby or child healthy and fighting fit. This simple fruit-filled lolly is an easy way to boost their intake of fruit as well as keeping them hydrated on a hot day. Unlike commercial lollies, there are no sugars or sweeteners – simply pure fruit!

2 oranges
1 large ripe mango, pitted and
   cut into chunks

1 Juice the oranges and pour the juice into a blender. Add the mango and process until smooth.
2 Pour the mixture into four or six lolly moulds, depending on size, and put in the freezer until set, around 3–4 hours or overnight.

MAKES 4–6

PREPARATION
10 minutes + freezing

STORAGE
Freeze the lollies for 1 month.

SERVE THIS WITH...
Tostada Chilli Wedges
  (see page 53)

HEALTH BENEFITS
Mangoes are packed with antioxidants, including vitamins C and E and beta-carotene, which is important for protecting the body against harmful free radicals and supporting immune function. Rich in soluble fibre and water, mangoes can improve digestive health and ease constipation. Beta-carotene helps to neutralize the harmful effects of UV light – useful for protecting the skin during the summer heat.

summer berry ice cups

SERVES 4

Scoops of this sensational dairy-free ice cream are served in little nut cases.

2 bananas, chopped
100g/3½oz/⅔ cup cashew nuts
200ml/7fl oz/generous ¾ cup
   pomegranate juice
225g/8oz/1¾ cups frozen mixed
   summer berries

NUT CUPS
160g/5½oz/1 cup cashew nuts
40g/1½oz/scant ½ cup
   desiccated coconut
60g/2¼oz/⅓ cup pitted dates
2 tbsp orange juice
light olive oil, for greasing

1 Freeze the bananas for 4 hours or overnight.

2 To make the nut cups, put the cashew nuts and coconut into a blender and blend until fine. Tip into a bowl.

3 Put the dates and orange juice into the blender and blend to a purée, adding water, if needed, to form a stiff paste.

4 Mix the date paste into the dry ingredients with your hands to form a crumbly dough.

5 Line four mini tart tins or cupcake tins with clear film. Lightly oil the clear film. Press the dough into the tins and leave to freeze for 1 hour to firm up. Remove from the tins.

6 To make the ice cream, put the cashew nuts and juice in a blender and process until creamy. Add the berries and bananas and process until they form a soft, smooth ice cream. Put a spoonful of ice cream in each nut cup.

PREPARATION
15 minutes + freezing

STORAGE
Keep the ice cream in the freezer for 1 month. Keep the nut cups in the fridge for 1 week or freeze for 1 month. Note that the recipe makes more ice cream than you will need for the cups.

SERVE THIS WITH...
Italian Tuna Balls (see page 106)

HEALTH BENEFITS
100% pure pomegranate juice is an easy way to boost your child's intake of powerful antioxidant compounds, including polyphenols and bioflavonoids, which, together with their high vitamin C content, help to support the body's immune system and protect brain cells from damage. These nutrients can also help to strengthen collagen, which is an essential component for healthy skin and bones.

ice cream sandwiches

Choc-mint ice cream served in chocolate wafers.
The coconut milk makes the ice cream dairy free.

MAKES 6

PREPARATION + COOKING
30 + 5 minutes + freezing
+ setting + softening

STORAGE
Freeze for up to 1 month.

SERVE THIS WITH...
Spicy Chicken Kebabs
 (see page 94)

HEALTH BENEFITS
Green superfood powders,
such as chlorella, spirulina,
wheatgrass and barley grass,
are all packed with chlorophyll,
amino acids and a whole range
of vitamins and minerals to
nourish children and keep
them energized. They are a
great addition to a child's diet,
especially if you are concerned
they do not eat sufficient greens
or if they are feeling low in
energy or have a poor appetite.

2 drops of peppermint extract
1 tsp green superfood powder
115g/4oz/¾ cup cashew nuts
3 mint leaves
200ml/7fl oz/generous ¾ cup
    coconut milk
2 tbsp raw cane sugar or xylitol
3 tbsp plain chocolate chips or
    cacao nibs

WAFERS
150g/5½oz dark chocolate
2 tbsp raw cane sugar or xylitol
1 tbsp olive oil or coconut oil
60g/2¼oz/½ cup chopped
    toasted nuts

1 Put all the ingredients for the ice cream, except the
chocolate chips, in a blender and blend on high until the
mixture is completely smooth. Stir in the chocolate chips.
2 Pour the mixture into six small ramekins and freeze
until firm, about 4 hours or overnight.
3 To make the wafers, melt the chocolate in a pan with
the sugar and olive oil, then stir in the nuts. Use a spoon
to form 12 circles of the mixture on a sheet of non-stick
baking parchment – the circles should be as big as the
ramekins. Leave for about 2 hours to set hard.
4 Remove the ice cream from the ramekins, put each one
on a wafer, then top with a second wafer. Leave to stand for
15 minutes before eating, so the ice cream softens slightly.

coconut jelly squares

Little squares of jelly on an oaty coconut base.

1 ripe mango, pitted and diced
2 passion fruit, pulp and juice
   only, seeds discarded
100–200ml/3½–7fl oz/scant
   ½ cup–generous ¾ cup
   apple juice (optional)
2 tbsp olive oil or coconut oil
4 tbsp vegetarian gelatine or
   agar agar flakes

BASE
light olive oil, for greasing
100g/3½oz/heaped 1 cup
   desiccated coconut
125g/4½oz/heaped 1¼ cups
   porridge oats
125g/4½oz/⅔ cup pitted dates
2 tbsp orange juice

1 Lightly grease and line a shallow 20cm/8in square tin.

2 To make the base, put the coconut and oats in a food processor and process to break down slightly. Add the dates and orange juice and continue to process to bring the mixture together.

3 Press into the prepared tin and freeze for 30 minutes.

4 To make the topping, put the mango and passion fruit in a blender and process until smooth. Make up the liquid, if needed, to 500ml/17fl oz/2 cups with apple juice.

5 Pour into a pan and add the olive oil. Sprinkle over the gelatine. Simmer for 5 minutes, stirring to dissolve.

6 Remove from the heat and leave to cool slightly.

7 Pour the jelly over the base and put in the fridge to set, about 3–4 hours or overnight. Cut into squares to serve.

MAKES 12–15

PREPARATION + COOKING
20 + 5 minutes + freezing
+ chilling

STORAGE
Keep in the fridge for 3–4 days.

SERVE THIS WITH...
Tandoori Chicken Strips
  (see page 44)
naan bread

HEALTH BENEFITS
A great energy booster, passion fruit is packed with B vitamins, iron, magnesium, vitamin C and fibre, which are all needed to maintain energy levels, support the nervous system and keep the brain and body fuelled, especially during times of stress. It is also a good source of vitamin A, which is important for maintaining healthy mucus membranes and skin.

peaches with berry syrup

HEALTH BENEFITS

Peaches and nectarines provide good sources of antioxidants, including carotenoids such as lycopene and lutein. These can help to protect against disease, support immune health and maintain healthy eyes and skin. Peaches also provide a useful source of potassium, which can help to maintain proper fluid balance and help regulate nerve and muscle activity.

This simple, summery dessert is delicious warm or cold. Cutting the peaches into wedges makes them a perfect finger food, and they are delicious dipped into the sweet strawberry syrup. You could also thread the wedges onto skewers and cook lightly over a barbecue.

4 ripe peaches, halved, pitted
    and thickly sliced
3 tbsp raw cane sugar or xylitol
225g/8oz strawberries
1 tbsp arrowroot or cornflour

1 Preheat the grill to high. Put some aluminium foil over a grill rack.
2 Put the peach slices on the grill rack and sprinkle with 2 tablespoons of the sugar.
3 Grill for 4–5 minutes until the wedges are golden brown.
4 Meanwhile, make the strawberry syrup by putting the strawberries, arrowroot and remaining sugar in a blender and blending until smooth. Pour into a small pan, and heat gently for 1–2 minutes, stirring all the time, until the sauce thickens slightly. Pour into a little bowl for dipping, and serve with the peach slices.

SERVES 4

PREPARATION + COOKING
15 + 7 minutes

STORAGE
Keep in the fridge for 1 day.

SERVE THIS WITH...
Beetroot & Beef Mini Burgers
  (see page 102)
mixed salad
wholemeal rolls

griddled pineapple

Pineapple skewers with orange coconut cream.

SERVES 6

PREPARATION + COOKING
15 + 15 minutes + soaking

STORAGE
Keep the pineapple in the fridge for 1 day and the cream for 3 days.

SERVE THIS WITH…
Coconut-Salmon Sticks with Tomato Chutney (see page 105) mixed salad

HEALTH BENEFITS
Calcium- and magnesium-rich foods such as tofu are important to relax nerve and muscle cells. A lack of either can make children irritable and nervous. If your child is on a dairy-free diet, make sure they eat plenty of nuts, seeds, calcium-enriched milk alternatives, leafy greens and beans, including soya, and tofu.

2 tsp arrowroot or cornflour
juice and finely grated zest of
    2 oranges
2 tbsp raw cane sugar or xylitol
1 small ripe pineapple,
    quartered, cored and sliced
    into thick wedges
light olive oil, for greasing

CREAM
225g/8oz silken tofu
50g/1¾oz/heaped ½ cup
    desiccated coconut

1 Soak 8 wooden skewers in water for 30 minutes.
2 Meanwhile, put the arrowroot in a small pan with a little of the orange juice and mix to form a smooth paste. Gradually mix in the remaining juice, then add the sugar and zest. Stir over a low heat for 2–3 minutes until the sugar dissolves and the sauce thickens slightly. Cool.
3 Set aside 150g/5½oz of the pineapple wedges, put the remainder in a shallow dish and pour over the orange sauce to coat. Thread 2 of pieces of pineapple onto each skewer.
4 Preheat and lightly grease a griddle pan with oil. Cook the pineapple skewers on the griddle pan in batches for 1–2 minutes on each side until golden brown.
5 Put the cream ingredients and reserved pineapple in a blender. Process until smooth. Pour into a bowl and serve with the pineapple. Remove the skewers before serving.

mango-orange crêpes

These fruity wholegrain pancakes are packed full of vitamins, and delicious too!

75g/2½oz/scant ⅔ cup plain flour
75g/2½oz/½ cup wholemeal flour
1 tbsp ground flaxseeds
finely grated zest of 2 oranges
3 eggs

330ml/11¼fl oz/1⅓ cups milk
2 tbsp olive oil or coconut oil

FILLING
2 mangoes, pitted and chopped
1 tbsp lemon juice
1 tbsp raw cane sugar or xylitol

1 To make the crêpes, put the flours, flaxseeds, orange zest, eggs and milk into a blender and process until smooth.
2 Heat half of the olive oil in a small crêpe or frying pan, then pour in a little batter and swirl it around. Cook over a high heat for 1–2 minutes until the top side is dry, then flip over and cook the underside briefly, about 1 minute. Remove from the pan and stack up, interleaved with parchment paper. Repeat with the remaining batter, adding the remaining oil to the pan if needed – the batter should make 8 crêpes.
3 To make the mango filling, put all the ingredients in a blender and process to form a thick purée.
4 Spread a little of the mango purée over each crêpe and roll up tightly. Slice into rounds and serve.

MAKES 8

PREPARATION + COOKING
15 + 25 minutes

STORAGE
Keep in the fridge for 2 days or freeze for up to 1 month.

SERVE THIS WITH…
Crispy Spiced Prawns (see page 58)

HEALTH BENEFITS
Flaxseeds, also known as linseeds, are one of the richest plant sources of omega-3 fatty acids – important for brain function, cell health and combating inflammation in the body. They are also high in soluble fibre, making them a useful remedy for easing constipation.

sweet cherry samosas

These triangles are filled with sweet cherries.

250g/9oz cherries, chopped
2 tbsp pure fruit cherry jam
70g/2½oz butter
12 filo pastry sheets, each cut
    to 6 x 25cm/2½ x 10in
raw cane sugar, for sprinkling

SHERBET DIP
8 mint leaves
4 tbsp raw cane sugar or xylitol
1 tbsp vitamin C powder
½ tsp bicarbonate of soda

1 Make the filling by mixing the cherries and jam in a bowl.
2 Preheat the oven to 200°C/400°F/Gas 6. Melt the butter
in a small pan, then lightly grease a baking sheet with it.
Line the sheet with baking parchment.
3 Spread out a sheet of filo pastry and brush with some
melted butter. Put another sheet on top and brush.
4 Put a small amount of the cherries on one end of the
strip, fold one corner of the pastry over the mixture to form
a triangle, then fold the remaining pastry over the top to
continue the triangle pattern. Repeat until all of the pastry
has been folded and you have a triangle-shaped samosa.
5 Put on the baking sheet, brush with butter and sprinkle
with sugar. Repeat with the remaining filo sheets to form
6 samosas. Bake for 10–15 minutes until golden.
6 Put all the sherbet dip ingredients in a blender and blend
until smooth. Put in a small bowl. Serve with the samosas.

lemon cheesecake

Creamy and utterly delicious.

light olive oil, for greasing
125g/4½oz/heaped ¾ cup
  cashew nuts
100g/3½oz/1 cup porridge oats
juice of ½ lemon
finely grated zest of 1 lemon
5 tbsp melted coconut oil
2 tbsp raw cane sugar or xylitol

TOPPING
225g/8oz Greek yogurt
350g/12oz cream cheese
2 eggs
juice and finely grated zest of
  2 lemons
2 tbsp plain flour
3 tbsp raw cane sugar or xylitol

1 Preheat the oven to 200°C/400°F/Gas 6. Grease a 20cm/
8in square shallow tin and line it with baking parchment.
2 Put the cashew nuts in a food processor and process
until finely ground. Add the porridge oats and pulse
lightly. Tip into a large bowl with the lemon juice and zest.
3 Heat the oil in a small pan with the sugar until warm,
then pour over the nuts and oats and stir to combine.
Spoon into the prepared tin and press down firmly.
4 Bake for 10 minutes until lightly firm, then remove from
the oven and leave to cool for 5 minutes. Reduce the heat
to 180°C/350°F/Gas 4.
5 Put the topping ingredients in a food processor and
process until smooth. Pour over the base and bake for
35–40 minutes, until the topping is set and lightly coloured.
Turn off the oven and leave inside to cool, then chill.

MAKES 15 SLICES

PREPARATION + COOKING
20 + 50 minutes + chilling
+ cooling

STORAGE
Keep in the fridge for 3 days.

SERVE THIS WITH...
Herby Koftas (see page 99)
wholemeal pittas

HEALTH BENEFITS
Greek yogurt has a mild creamy
taste that young children adore,
but opt for natural yogurt only
as most fruit yogurts are laden
with sugar and sweeteners. Look
for authentic Greek yogurt rather
than 'Greek style', which often
contains thickeners or stabilizers
to create a thicker texture and
increase shelf life. When choosing
a brand, the fewer ingredients in
the yogurt the better. Look for
natural yogurt, which contains
just milk or milk and cream and
live active yogurt culture.

banana choc-nut bites

Choc-nut bananas in crispy filo pastry.

SERVES 4

PREPARATION + COOKING
15 + 10 minutes

STORAGE
Keep in the fridge for 1 day.

SERVE THIS WITH...
Italian Tuna Balls (see page 106)

HEALTH BENEFITS
Bananas are a well-known energizing fruit, containing natural sugars and B vitamins, which the body needs to produce energy. Vitamins B5 and B6 also help support the nervous system and combat the effects of stress. Bananas are a great mood booster, too, being a natural source of the amino acid tryptophan, which the body converts into the "feel good" neurotransmitter serotonin.

light olive oil, for greasing
2 tbsp cashew nut butter
50g/2oz dark chocolate, grated

8 sheets of filo pastry
30g/1oz butter
2 bananas, chopped

1 Preheat the oven to 200°C/400°F/Gas 6. Lightly grease two baking sheets with oil and line with baking parchment.
2 Mix together the cashew nut butter and chocolate.
3 Put 2 sheets of filo on a board, one on top of each other. Melt the butter in a small pan, then brush the top filo sheet with melted butter.
4 Put a quarter of the banana lengthways in the centre of the pastry, leaving a 2cm/¾in gap at the sides. Top with a quarter of the chocolate mixture.
5 Fold in both sides of the pastry, then roll up to enclose the filling. Put seam-side down on one of the baking sheets. Repeat with the remaining filo sheets to make 4 parcels. Brush with butter and bake for 10 minutes.

frozen blueberry & chocolate slice

A great celebration dessert for parties.

3 tbsp melted coconut oil
125g/4½oz/heaped ¾ cup
  cashew nuts
150g/5½oz/1 cup blueberries,
  fresh or frozen
finely grated zest of 1 lemon
1 tbsp lemon juice
250ml/9fl oz/1 cup grape juice
  or other berry juice
1 tbsp cocoa powder (optional)

BASE
light olive oil, for greasing
140g/5oz/scant 1 cup almonds
1 tbsp ground flaxseeds
1 tsp cinnamon
a pinch of salt
1 tbsp cocoa powder
75g/2½oz/scant ⅔ cup raisins
1 tsp pure vanilla extract
6 tbsp melted coconut oil

1 Lightly grease a 20cm/8in square cake tin with oil and line it with baking parchment.

2 For the base, put the almonds, flaxseeds, cinnamon, salt and cocoa powder in a food processor and process to form small crumbs. Add the raisins and vanilla extract.

3 Pour the oil into the mixture and process again until the mixture forms a dough. Press into the tin and leave to chill while you make the filling.

4 Pour the oil into a blender. Add the remaining ingredients and blend until smooth. Pour over the base. Freeze for 4 hours before cutting into slices.

MAKES 12 SLICES

PREPARATION + COOKING
20 minutes + 4 minutes
+ freezing

STORAGE
Freeze for up to 1 month.

SERVE THIS WITH…
Crispy Chicken (see page 92)

HEALTH BENEFITS
Blueberries are a wonderful superfood for your child's brain, bursting with powerful protective and immune-supporting antioxidants, including anthocyanidins, vitamin C and E, selenium and zinc. Zinc is an essential mineral to help the brain turn glucose into energy as well as being needed for the production of hormones and neurotransmitters for brain function.

*fruit slice

HEALTH BENEFITS
Raspberries are bursting with vitamins and antioxidants to help protect the body's cells and tissues against damage. They are a good source of B vitamins, including folate and niacin, which are important for the production of neurotransmitters to aid brain function. They also contain lots of soluble fibre, which, together with the protein from the nuts, will help to keep blood sugar levels even through the day.

This delicious moist tart can be enjoyed hot or cold and has a low glycaemic index to help keep blood sugar levels even throughout the day. It contains no wheat or gluten and is packed with protein, calcium, magnesium and fibre. The eggs provide memory-boosting nutrients.

light olive oil, for greasing
2 ripe pears, cored and diced
3 eggs, separated
4 tbsp raw cane sugar or xylitol
250g/9oz/2½ cups ground
 almonds

1 tsp cinnamon
1 tsp gluten-free baking powder
200g/7oz/2 cups frozen
 raspberries

MAKES 12

PREPARATION + COOKING
20 + 40 minutes

STORAGE
Keep in the fridge for 3 days
or freeze for up to 1 month.

SERVE THIS WITH...
Tapas Soufflé Omelette
 (see page 118)
mixed salad

1 Preheat the oven to 180°C/350°F/Gas 4. Lightly grease a 20 x 30cm/8 x 12in shallow tin with oil and line it with baking parchment.

2 Put the pears, egg yolks and sugar in a food processor and process until thick and creamy. Add the ground almonds, cinnamon and baking powder and process until combined.

3 Put the egg whites in a bowl and whisk with an electric hand mixer until stiff peaks form. Carefully fold the egg whites into the pear mixture, then add the raspberries.

4 Pour the mixture into the prepared baking tin. Bake for 30–40 minutes until golden and firm to touch. Leave to cool in the tin before cutting into slices.

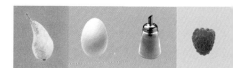

frozen pineapple cheesecake slice

A lovely tropical-flavoured frozen bar.

SERVES 10–12

PREPARATION
20 minutes + freezing

STORAGE
Keep in the fridge for 3 days
or freeze for up to 1 month.

SERVE THIS WITH...
Risotto Cheese Balls
  (see page 111)
mixed salad

HEALTH BENEFITS
Pineapple is rich in the protein-
digesting enzyme bromelain,
which promotes healthy
digestion and may help to ease
constipation. As it is able to
break down areas of inflamed
body tissue, pineapple can
help reduce inflammation and
swelling making it useful for
alleviating symptoms associated
with conditions such as asthma.
Eating pineapple between meals
maximizes bromelain's anti-
inflammatory effect.

light olive oil, for greasing
250ml/9fl oz/1 cup coconut milk
75g/2¾oz/1½ cup cashew nuts
300g/10½oz pineapple, cored
    and cut into chunks
2 tbsp raw cane sugar or xylitol
finely grated zest of 1 lime
1 tbsp lime juice

BASE
125g/4½oz/1 cup walnut pieces
60g/2¼oz/½ cup cashew nuts
50ml/1¾fl oz/scant ¼ cup
    melted coconut oil
3 tbsp ground flaxseed
finely grated zest of 1 lime
60g/2¼oz/⅓ cup pitted dates,
    chopped
1 tbsp raw cane sugar or xylitol

1 Lightly grease a 20cm/8in square shallow tin with oil
and line it with baking parchment.

2 To make the base, put the walnuts and cashew nuts
in a food processor and process to form fine crumbs.
Add the coconut oil to the processor with the remaining
ingredients and process to form a crumbly mixture.

3 Press the mixture into the prepared tin and leave to chill.

4 To make the filling, put all the ingredients into a blender
and blend until thick and creamy. Pour over the base and
freeze for at least 3 hours.

5 Remove from the freezer 30 minutes before serving.

apple & pecan tarts

These tarts have a spiced apple and raisin filling.

2 cooking apples, peeled,
    cored and roughly chopped
1 tsp cinnamon
2 tbsp raw cane sugar or xylitol
1 handful of raisins

BASE
250g/9oz/2½ cups pecans
100g/3½oz/1 cup porridge oats
1 tsp cinnamon
60g/2¼oz/⅓ cup pitted dates,
    chopped
juice of 1 orange

MAKES 6

PREPARATION + COOKING
20 + 5 minutes

STORAGE
Keep in the fridge for 2–3 days.

SERVE THIS WITH…
Crispy Pork Belly Bites
  (see page 97)

HEALTH BENEFITS
Dates are naturally sweet and energizing, but thanks to their fibre content they can also help to moderate the speed at which they release their sugars into the bloodstream. They are a perfect pick-me-up after exercise, especially when combined with some protein such as a handful of nuts. A good source of iron and magnesium, they can be useful when children are feeling tired or fatigued.

1 To make the tart base, put the pecans in a food processor and process until finely ground. Add the oats and process to break up slightly. Tip into a bowl and stir in the cinnamon.

2 Put the dates and orange juice in a blender and blend to form a paste. Add to the oat mixture and mix with your hands to form a crumbly dough.

3 Press the dough into six little tart cases or holes in a cupcake tin.

4 To make the filling, put the apples, cinnamon and sugar in a pan with a splash of water and gently cook for 4 minutes until soft. Mash with a potato masher to form a chunky pureé. Remove from the heat and stir in the raisins. Allow the mixture to cool, then spoon into the tart cases. Remove the tarts from the tin and serve.

menu plans

wheat- & gluten-free 5-day menu

Many of the recipes in this book are suitable for those on a wheat- or gluten-free diet or who are wishing to reduce their intake of wheat and gluten, which can be common allergies in children. If your child is a coeliac, a lifelong exclusion of all gluten grains (wheat, barley, rye and contaminated oats) is essential. However, you will find many delicious, safe options for your child in this book.

Day 1

Breakfast: Raisin Quinoa Slices (see page 28) and fresh fruit

Lunch: Crispy Spiced Prawns (see page 58) and crudités; fresh fruit and yogurt

Dinner: Thai-Spiced Turkey Balls (see page 95) with rice and vegetables; Frozen Pineapple Cheesecake Slice (see page 138)

Snacks: Roasted Red Pepper & Almond Dip (see page 69) with vegetable sticks; Lemon-Coconut Macaroons (see page 78)

Day 2

Breakfast: Almond & Apricot Scotch Pancakes (see page 30)

Lunch: Peanut Chicken Bites (see page 42), crudités and salad; fresh fruit and nuts

Dinner: Italian Tuna Balls (using gluten-free breadcrumbs and flour) (see page 106), vegetables; Peaches with Berry Syrup (see page 128)

Snacks: nuts; Date & Spice Muffins (see page 24)

Day 3

Breakfast: Crunchy Granola Bites (see
   page 25) (using gluten-free oats); fruit
Lunch: Tandoori Chicken (see page 44) with
   rice cakes, baby corn and sugarsnap peas;
   fresh fruit and yogurt
Dinner: Greek Rissoles (see page 100)
   (using gluten-free breadcrumbs), salad;
   Summer Berry Ice Cups (see page 125)
Snacks: Almond Linzer Biscuits (see
   page 75); fresh fruit and seeds

Day 4

Breakfast: Vegetable Rostis with Herby
   Cottage Cheese (see page 34)
Lunch: Fruity Salmon Skewers (see page 54),
   raw vegetables; Mango Fruit Lollies
   (see page 124)
Dinner: Pork Satay Sticks (see page 98) with
   rice and vegetables; Apple & Pecan Tarts
   (using gluten-free oats) (see page 139)
Snacks: Chocolate Cupcakes (see page 76);
   fresh fruit and nuts

Day 5

Breakfast: Omelette Roll-Ups (see page 38)
Lunch: Tofu & Cashew Burgers (see page 60)
   in a gluten-free roll with salad; fresh fruit
   and yogurt
Dinner: Polenta Fish Cakes (see page 108),
   vegetables; Frozen Blueberry & Chocolate
   Slice (see page 135)
Snacks: Courgette & Apple Cake (see page
   84); fresh fruit and seeds

vegetarian 5-day menu

Ensuring your child gets sufficient protein, iron, zinc, calcium, magnesium and essential omega-3 fats is particularly important if they are following a vegetarian diet. Include a variety of grains, pulses, beans, eggs and dairy produce as well as nuts and seeds to ensure sufficient protein and mineral intake. Focus on a range of vegetables daily, including dark green leafy vegetables such as spinach, broccoli and kale for iron, and accompany with vitamin C-rich foods like fresh fruit to enhance absorption. This menu plan is free from meat, poultry, fish and seafood. Check labels to make sure any cheeses are vegetarian.

Day 1

Breakfast: Cranberry Seed Bread (see page 22) with nut butter

Lunch: Tofu & Cashew Burgers (see page 60) in a roll with salad; fresh fruit and yogurt

Dinner: Vegetable Samosas (see page 112), spinach and peas; Griddled Pineapple (see page 130)

Snacks: Choc-nut Lemon Bars (see page 81); Teriyaki Mixed Seeds (see page 86)

Day 2

Breakfast: Tomato Bagel Melts (see page 36)

Lunch: Cheese & Sundried Tomato Polenta Toasts (see page 64) with crudités; Peaches with Berry Syrup (see page 128)

Dinner: Crispy Tofu Skewers (see page 114), rice cakes and broccoli spears; Fruit Slice (see page 136)

Snacks: nuts and fresh fruit; Apricot Oat Slices (see page 80)

Day 3

Breakfast: Berry Blinis with Sweet Cherry Sauce (see page 29)

Lunch: Babaganoush with Pitta Triangles (see page 61) with salad; Almond Chocolate Butter on Apple Wedges (see page 73)

Dinner: Tapas Soufflé Omelette (see page 118); Frozen Pineapple Cheesecake Slice (see page 138)

Snacks: Pumpkin Seed Buns (see page 85); fresh fruit and seeds

Day 4

Breakfast: Chocolate Peanut Waffles (see page 32) with fruit

Lunch: Easy Sushi Rolls (see page 57), rice cakes; fresh fruit and yogurt

Dinner: Risotto Cheese Balls (see page 111), sweetcorn and carrots; Coconut Jelly Squares (see page 127)

Snacks: fresh fruit with nut butter; Teriyaki Mixed Seeds (see page 86)

Day 5

Breakfast: Tropical Breakfast Bars (see page 26)

Lunch: Creamy Dips (see page 69) and Chunky Breadsticks (see page 87); Fruit Slice (see page 136)

Dinner: Mini Vegetable Quiches (see page 119) and salad; Summer Berry Ice Cups (see page 125)

Snacks: yogurt and fruit; nuts or seeds

INDEX